**NEW DIRECTIONS
FOR CONTINUING
EDUCATION**

Number 10 • 1981

NEW DIRECTIONS FOR CONTINUING EDUCATION

A Quarterly Sourcebook
Alan B. Knox, Editor-in-Chief

Number 10, 1981

Advising and Counseling Adult Learners

WITHDRAWN

Frank R. DiSilvestro
Editor

Jossey-Bass Inc., Publishers
San Francisco • Washington • London

ADVISING AND COUNSELING ADULT LEARNERS
New Directions for Continuing Education
Number 10, 1981
    Frank R. DiSilvestro, Editor

New Directions for Continuing Education (publication number
USPS 493-930) quarterly by Jossey-Bass Inc., Publishers.
Subscriptions are available at the regular rate for institutions,
libraries, and agencies of $30 for one year. Individuals may
subscribe at the special professional rate of $18 for one year.
Second-class postage rates paid at San Francisco, California,
and at additional mailing offices.

Correspondence:
Subscriptions, single-issue orders, change of address notices,
undelivered copies, and other correspondence should be sent to
New Directions Subscriptions, Jossey-Bass Inc., Publishers,
433 California Street, San Francisco, California 94104.

Editorial correspondence should be sent to the Editor-in-Chief,
Alan B. Knox, Office for the Study of Continuing Professional
Education, University of Illinois at Urbana–Champaign,
Urbana, Illinois 61801.

Library of Congress Catalogue Card Number LC 80-84268
International Standard Serial Number ISSN 0195-2242
International Standard Book Number ISBN 87589-817-3

Cover design by Willi Baum
Manufactured in the United States of America

Contents

Editor's Notes

With increasing numbers of adults interested in continuing education or career transitions, there has been a concomitant increase in the need for counseling. The purpose of this sourcebook, therefore, is to describe counseling services that assist adults with their educational and career planning. Such counseling services include efforts by people such as counselors, teachers, and administrators, which take place in settings as varied as colleges and universities, business and industry, communities, and the military.

This sourcebook is a resource for practitioners who would like to establish or revise counseling programs for adult learners, provides ideas for improving counseling skills in dealing with adult learners, and suggests topics for research concerning the types of skills needed by those who counsel adult learners and those who teach counselors of adult learners.

Chapter One provides an overview of literature and information sources of interest to practitioners involved in counseling adult learners. One of the most significant innovations in counseling adult learners is the community-based education guidance center. In Chapter Two, Diana Ironside describes four community-based centers and discusses aspects of them that can be transferred to other areas.

The next two chapters offer different perspectives on counseling adult learners in the workplace, one from labor and another from management. Levine and Piggins, in Chapter Three, address the need of workers to pursue various kinds of education and training. They describe how a workplace counselor can help workers gain greater access to information, training, and educational opportunities in order to better deal with work and personal changes. In Chapter Four, Ludeman describes how the provision of counseling by management in a bank helps employees engage in self-directed learning to gain personal satisfaction and attain corporate goals.

Chapters Five, Six, and Seven deal with counseling adults returning to higher education. Chapter Five focuses on the identification of adult student needs in community colleges. In that chapter, Mangano and Corrado describe the implications for counselors of adults in community colleges of the results of their reentry adult needs assessment and satisfaction study. Chapter Six, by Nowak and Shriberg, describes how knowledge of adult learning and development can help a university respond better to counseling needs of adult students. In Chapter Seven, Gelling provides a case example of how effective counseling services in a continuing education division help attract and retain adult students.

Descriptions of counselors serving adult learners in diverse settings are continued in the next four chapters. Cotzin and Radcliffe, in Chapter Eight, describe adult educational and career counseling services for skilled and unskilled workers in a large hospital. In Chapter Nine, Brenner describes how an effective counseling program can help meet the diverse educational needs of military personnel. DiSilvestro and Williams, in Chapter Ten, deal with the need for adult counseling in the public schools, and how such counseling can be provided in light of limited financial support. In Chapter Eleven, Arbeiter examines current career counseling services for adults and explores further possibilities utilizing computers and view screens.

The next two chapters describe innovative approaches to counseling adult learners. In Chapter Twelve, Rayman describes current and potential uses of computers in adult guidance and counseling. In Chapter Thirteen, Wertheim describes nontraditional approaches to helping adult learners and questions the extent to which those approaches offer meaningful counseling. Knox, in the final chapter, summarizes emerging issues related to counseling adult learners and provides a glimpse into likely future directions for this important service to adults.

Helping adult learners with educational, career, and personal development is a fulfilling and extremely worthwhile experience. I wish to thank our sourcebook authors, whose articles will contribute significantly to greater practitioner proficiency and program services for adult learners.

Frank R. DiSilvestro
Editor

Frank R. DiSilvestro, assistant professor of continuing studies at Indiana University, teaches the graduate course "Counseling the Adult Learner." He was chairman of the National University Continuing Education Association (NUCEA) Student Services Division and currently is a member of the NUCEA Board of Directors.

Useful resources exist to help counselors increase their knowledge and
improve their performance in counseling adult learners.

Perspectives on Counseling Adult Learners

Frank R. DiSilvestro

Interest in counseling for adults who wish to continue learning is increasing. This interest may be in response to the growing number of students over age twenty-five enrolled at our postsecondary institutions (Miller, 1979–1980) and to increasing numbers of students enrolled in adult secondary and basic education programs (National Association for Public Continuing and Adult Education, 1980). It may also be due to the realization that adults experience significant changes and need opportunities for continued personal growth.

The purpose of such counseling is described by Knox and Farmer (1977, p. 390) as follows: "The purpose of counseling services is to assist adult learners in exploring personal aspirations and available opportunities and to make plans related to their educational development." The number and diversity of publications now addressing the topic of counseling adult learners can be bewildering. Designed to give the practitioner some direction in utilizing this information, this chapter points out selected sources that provide an overview and a focused perspective on counseling adult learners.

An Overview

This sourcebook describes various methods of counseling adult learners, and various settings where such counseling occurs. Because of this diversity, an overview of related information that can be applied across methods and settings might be helpful. In a selective review of literature dealing with counseling the adult learner, Goldberg (1980) provides perspectives on five areas: (1) the need for counseling adult learners, (2) meeting the adult learner's specific needs, (3) life-span development, (4) new forms of counseling services, and (5) new approaches and techniques for counseling adults.

Utilizing a computer search of the ERIC data base from 1966 through 1978, Zawada and Walz (1980) focus on educational and vocational counseling. They include descriptions of numerous counseling approaches and techniques, as well as model programs and projects, program evaluation, and implications for counselor training. A related source, by Walz and Benjamin (1980), deals with adult counseling for life transitions. The first in a series of publications by ERIC/CAPS on the topic of adult counseling, it reviews basic concepts about adult development and trends in adult counseling. A second volume, due in 1981, will analyze both adult counseling programs and adult counselor training, while a third volume, due in 1982, will describe a multistage model for the development and installation of adult counseling programs in a variety of settings. Additional topics, such as theoretical considerations in counseling adults, adult development and its relation to counseling intervention, emerging adult counseling programs, and adult counselor training, are discussed by Schlossberg and Entine (1977).

A report issued by the University of Southern California (1978) focused on the relation of counseling and information services to adult education; primary, secondary, and higher education; personnel and training; and the organization and administration of such services. The most comprehensive descriptions of counseling and information services for adult learners are provided by Knox and Farmer (1977), Ironside (1976), and Ironside and Jacobs (1977). These three sources describe the many ways adults are assisted in identifying and selecting the learning activities they pursue.

A Focused Perspective

The settings and methods described in this sourcebook focus on three areas: the application of knowledge about adult development and learning to counseling adult learners, educational and career counseling for adult learners, and the translation of these issues into adult counseling skills.

Adult Development and Learning. Knowledge of adult development and learning is extremely helpful for people who counsel adult learners. Heffernan, Macy, and Vickers (1976) indicate that for counselors it is the counterpart to content mastery for teachers. Such knowledge can be applied to the delivery methods and settings described in this sourcebook. In a comprehensive analysis of adult development and learning, Knox (1977) describes research related to family role performance, education, work and community performance, physical condition, personality, women's roles, and adjusting to changing events. Knox (1979) also discusses the relationship of adult mid-life changes to educational programming and career planning. Troll (1975) describes research findings with direct applications to counseling adult learners. She addresses topics such as physical, intellectual, and personal development during early and middle adulthood, as well as adult development in the family and in the job world. A recent report on adult development and approaches to learning by the National Institute of Education (1980) further explores the idea of adulthood as a period of continuing change with implications for adult learning. Understanding these changes can help counselors understand adults' motivations for pursuing further education or career changes, as well as some of the difficulties the individual learner may have in relating to these experiences. The report emphasizes the importance of recognizing the diversity of adult learners and learning.

Educational and Career Counseling. Educational and career counseling are very closely tied together. In a study about Americans in transition, Aslanian and Bricknell (1980) relate that adults often participate in education in order to cope with changes in their lives—career, family, or leisure transitions that require further learning. Darkenwald (1980) advocates alternative models of delivering educational and career guidance for adults, such as community-based or institutional consortium-based models. He describes these approaches and indicates that they are essential in order to avoid marginal delivery of guidance and informational services. Ironside (1976) provides a comprehensive source for educational counseling of adults. She includes information about counseling and testing, learner needs, and the use and dissemination of educational information. Cross (1978) provides additional assistance to practitioners by describing ways of connecting adult learners to particular learning resources.

In the area of higher education, three sources seem particularly helpful to adult counselors. Shriberg (1980) provides information designed to alert higher education to the needs of the returning adult student, including descriptions of how to adjust student services to meet the needs of the adult learner. Kasworm's (1980) research and descriptions are related to student services for older undergraduate students. The College Board's (1979) descriptions of numerous ways in which colleges are serving adult learners provide examples for counselors of adults in that setting.

Two extremely helpful studies dealing with adult career development and guidance were conducted by the National Center for Research in Vocational Education. The first study examined the theoretical literature that pertains to career counseling for adults and reviewed alternative ways to deliver career guidance. The results, edited by Campbell and Shaltry (n.d.), describe the context, theories, clients, and programs concerned with career guidance for adults. The second study, by the National Center for Research in Vocational Education (1979), investigated the dimensions and parameters of career planning and adjustment problems over the life span and described a diagnostic taxonomy of those problems. The taxonomy consisted of four problem areas: career decision making, implementing career plans, organizational/institutional performance, and organizational/institutional adaptation. Both sources provide valuable assistance to counselors of adult learners and help to strengthen the practitioner's skills in career counseling and program organization.

Adult Counseling Skills. The translation of knowledge and issues into effective practices is the keystone of counseling adult learners. Adults are different from adolescents and children, and counseling proficiencies and services should respond to the unique and diverse characteristics of adult learners. Schlossberg, Troll, and Leibowitz (1978) provide an invaluable resource dealing with specific adult counseling issues and corresponding proficiencies and activities. Many activities can be performed by an individual working alone, while others can be utilized in a group setting. The reference section cites excellent sources for further readings. In a related source, Waters and others (1977) describe strategies for educating adult counselors, focusing on an eclectic model developed to educate paraprofessionals at their Continuum Center for Adult Counseling and Leadership Training. Their program is particularly applicable to this sourcebook because it utilizes several less academic approaches to prepare counselors to work with adults in various settings.

Two additional sources can assist counselors with their skills and help provide solutions to problem situations encountered by adult learners. The first, a set of materials designed through the Northwest Regional Educational Laboratory (1975) to assist counselors of adults, provides both information and competency-based skill training in a variety of areas, including group counseling, retirement and leisure counseling, career development, interracial understanding, identification of community resources, design and coordination of an adult counseling and guidance program, retention and follow-up of adult students, and selection of assessment instruments. Riggs (1980) designed a very useful pamphlet for practitioners in academic settings, health professionals, social workers, and business and industry training directors involved with advising and counseling adults. She describes typical problems encountered by adult learners and provides alternate solutions in areas such as self-understanding, educational and career planning, personal problem solving, advocacy, and referral.

A Final Note

Many additional sources relating to counseling adult learners appear in the references cited here and in the following sourcebook articles. Practitioners can greatly enhance their counseling effectiveness by utilizing those references which relate most directly to the needs of their own clientele and setting. This chapter and the remaining chapters both illustrate the diverse considerations involved in counseling adult learners and provide direction and assistance in helping practitioners more effectively counsel adult learners.

References

Aslanian, C. B., and Bricknell, H. M. *Americans in Transition: Life Changes as Reasons for Adult Learning*. New York: The College Board, 1980.

Campbell, R. E., and Shaltry, P. (Eds.). *Perspectives on Adult Career Development and Guidance*. Columbus, Ohio: National Center for Research in Vocational Education, n.d.

The College Board. *Three Hundred and Fifty Ways Colleges Are Serving Adult Learners.* New York: The College Board, 1979.

Cross, K. P. *The Missing Link: Connecting Adult Learners to Learning Resources.* New York: The College Board, 1978.

Darkenwald, G. G. "Educational and Career Guidance for Adults: Delivery System Alternatives." *The Vocational Guidance Quarterly,* 1980. *28* (2), 200–207.

Goldberg, J. C. "Counseling the Adult Learner: A Selective Review of the Literature." *Adult Education,* 1980, *30* (2), 67–81.

Heffernan, J. M., Macy, F. V., and Vickers, D. F. *Educational Brokering: A New Service for Adult Learners.* Syracuse, N.Y.: National Center for Educational Brokering, 1976.

Ironside, D. J. *Counseling and Information Services for Adult Learners in North America.* Bulletin of the International Bureau of Education. Paris: UNESCO, 1976.

Ironside, D. J., and Jacobs, D. E. *Trends in Counselling and Information Services for the Adult Learner.* Toronto: Ontario Institute for Studies in Education, 1977.

Kasworm, C. E. "Student Services for the Older Undergraduate Student." *Journal of College Student Personnel,* 1980, *21* (2), 163–169.

Knox, A. B. *Adult Development and Learning: A Handbook on Individual Growth and Competence in the Adult Years for Education and the Helping Professions.* San Francisco: Jossey-Bass, 1977.

Knox, A. B. (Ed.). *New Directions for Continuing Education: Programming for Adults Facing Mid-Life Change,* no. 2. San Francisco: Jossey-Bass, 1979.

Knox, A. B., and Farmer, H. S. "Overview of Counseling and Information Services for Adult Learners." *International Review of Education,* 1977, *23* (4), 387–414.

Miller, R. H. "A Decade of Data on Adult Learners." *The College Board Review,* 1979–1980, *114,* 16–17.

National Association for Public Continuing and Adult Education. *Public Continuing and Adult Education Almanac.* Yearbook. Washington, D.C.: National Association for Public Continuing and Adult Education, 1980.

National Center for Research in Vocational Education. *A Diagnostic Taxonomy of Adult Career Problems.* Columbus, Ohio: National Center for Research in Vocational Education, 1979.

National Institute of Education. *Adult Development and Approaches to Learning.* Washington, D.C.: National Institute of Education, 1980.

Northwest Regional Educational Laboratory. *Skills for Adult Guidance Educators.* Portland, Ore.: Northwest Regional Educational Laboratory, 1975.

Riggs, J. A. *Advising or Counseling Adults.* Readings in Program Development, no. 4. Urbana–Champaign: Office of Continuing Education and Public Service, University of Illinois, 1980.

Schlossberg, N. K., and Entine, A. D. (Eds.). *Counseling Adults.* Monterey, Calif.: Brooks/Cole, 1977.

Schlossberg, N. K., Troll, L. E., and Leibowitz, Z. *Perspectives on Counseling Adults.* Monterey, Calif.: Brooks/Cole, 1978.

Shriberg, A. (Ed.). *New Directions for Student Services: Providing Student Services for the Adult Learner,* no. 11. San Francisco: Jossey-Bass, 1980.

Troll, L. E. *Early and Middle Adulthood.* Monterey, Calif.: Brooks/Cole, 1975.

University of Southern California. *Ways and Means of Strengthening Information and Counseling Services for Adult Learners.* Los Angeles: College of Continuing Education, University of Southern California, 1978.

Walz, G. R., and Benjamin, L. *Counseling Adults for Life Transitions.* Ann Arbor, Mich.: ERIC Counseling and Personnel Services Clearinghouse, 1980.

Waters, E., and others. "Strategies for Training Adult Counselors." In N. K. Schlossberg and A. D. Entine (Eds.), *Counseling Adults.* Monterey, Calif.: Brooks/Cole, 1977.

Zawada, M. A., and Walz, G. R. *Counseling Adults.* Ann Arbor, Mich.: ERIC Counseling and Personnel Services Clearinghouse, 1980.

6

Frank R. DiSilvestro, assistant professor of continuing studies at Indiana University, teaches the graduate course "Counseling the Adult Learner." He was chairman of the National University Continuing Education Association (NUCEA) Student Services Division and currently is a member of the NUCEA Board of Directors.

Community-based models for counseling adults about new careers,
education, and life goals present exciting new opportunities for adult
learning and development.

Community Counseling
for Adults

Diana J. Ironside

One of the more pervasive and imporant innovations of adult educational
practice in the seventies must be the community-based education guidance
and information center, a service that specializes in counseling adults about
learning opportunities. While most visible in the United States, with some 300
centers, similar organizations now exist in many other countries. In fact, one
European center predates the seventies and may have pioneered the concept.

In 1978 and 1979, the author visited various communities in North
America and Europe in search of models for counseling adults about new
careers, educational options, and life goals. Two Canadian centers (Brantford
and Vancouver) and two European centers (Belfast and Cologne) were selected
for detailed study and for comparison of their organizational structures,
administrative styles, and staffing patterns. This chapter describes the four
centers and discusses how they exemplify aspects of a variety of models for
organizing counseling services.

First some models discussed in the recent literature are reviewed and
the origin and services of the four centers outlined (Ironside, 1980). Then the
characteristics of the models exhibited by the centers and the strengths and
weaknesses of each model are analyzed in relation to the key differences
among them, using illustrations from the individual centers' experiences.

In a useful study published by the University of California, Paltridge,
Regan, and Terkla (1979) examined various community support systems set

up to aid adult students in mid-career transition. From demographic and other descriptive data of seven communities in rural, urban, and metropolitan areas, the investigators detected four distinct forms of organization working to expand continuing education opportunities for adults. Using these data and returns from a comprehensive questionnaire survey of mid-career students, they constructed four models as a basis for community planning. These alternative models are strongly oriented to the user of education rather than to needs or interests of the providers of educational services. Some form of each model had been found that successfully created an environment in which continuing education thrived in the communities studied.

The first model specified an organization of a community council that was composed primarily of lay citizens representing the community and every educational, training, or learning resource. The second model consisted of an existing consortium of all the education/training providers in the community. The third model was the independent educational brokering agency, which provided information dissemination and adult career counseling, education program planning, and advice about appropriate educational institutions. The fourth model consisted of a network of all support services in the community that provide education and training and those which serve the adult population of prospective students, for example, welfare and employment agencies, regional economic planning commissions, industrial and labor councils, and so forth. Another model, while not considered ideal, was found to work well in several communities that they visited—the institutionally sponsored organization or center. Here the institution assumed a community-wide function of providing counseling and information on careers and education for adult learners.

A British study (Advisory Council for Adult and Continuing Education, 1979) described the three major types of operational structures of educational guidance services that prevail in the United Kingdom at present. These structures were the link chain, which relied on volunteer counselors or other professionals who acted as a referral network; the center, in which a centralized service with trained staff offered professional advice; and the link chain center, which combined the positive features of the other two.

Another model may exist in centers sponsored entirely or mainly by state or municipal governments. The best examples of this type are in the Federal Republic of Germany; descriptions appear in the author's case study of the Cologne Centre and in Peter Clyne's account (1979) of his visit to three counseling centers for underprivileged groups. While users may perceive centers as government services, their staffs seem to embrace a client-centered philosophy and to act as client advocates. The source of their income does not appear to affect the quality of service.

On close scrutiny of model three, it appears that independent community-based services may emphasize the advocacy function in a unique way, thereby adding a dimension that other models do not exhibit so persistently. The author's paper to the 1978 International Round Table for the Advancement of Counselling (Ironside, 1979) identified the role of client advocacy in breaking down institutional barriers that hinder adults' progress toward their learning goals (for example, poor course scheduling or prohibitive fees). While many services assist individual clients as advocates on a case basis, acting as advocate for adult learners as a group or serving as a facilitating agent for raising issues and for social and institutional change has been less common. One American broker, the Regional Learning Service (RLS) of central New York, set out to discover how it could be more effective in helping reduce barriers to adult students in postsecondary education. At the end of its year-long study (Riffer, 1978), RLS concluded that the skills needed to perform group advocacy are not the same as those needed to counsel individual clients. What is essential in group advocacy is an ability to work at the system level. The combination of group and individual client advocacy seems to be an increasingly important aspect of the broker model.

The Models in Action

Some of the unique aspects of the four centers discussed briefly here derive from the characteristics of the model or from the organizing principle of the individual center. Particular centers probably would have quite dissimilar features had their founding structures or principles been different. A short description of each center is followed by a discussion of the variations among them and an assessment of the strengths and weaknesses of the models they represent.

Women's Resources Center (WRC). Vancouver, the largest city of British Columbia, has a population close to half a million. It is served by two provincial universities and a variety of community colleges, specialized institutes, continuing education programs of school boards, among many others. In 1975–1976, nearly 341,000 adults across the province were engaged in continuing education, in public institutions alone.

The Women's Resources Center is a downtown drop-in center sponsored and funded by the University of British Columbia to serve the needs of women returning to education, reentering the labor force, or seeking a new life direction. WRC is located in two large rooms above shops on a busy street near the city center. Its director is also a staff member of the Centre for Continuing Education. The only other professional staff member is a half-time volunteer coordinator trainer; the balance of the staff are trained peer counselors called volunteer associates. Services include drop-in reception; information about learning resources and opportunities; vocational planning and job-hunting assistance; a life planning service with individual interviews and groups; psychological testing; discussion groups; and educational programs, courses, and workshops tailored to the needs of women.

An extensive training program has been developed for the volunteers, including a core of fifteen hours on the theory and practice of counseling and six hours each on the areas of vocational planning, learning resources/information bank, and the relationships among health, nutrition, stress management, and psychic functions. Recent client surveys indicate that over half of the women who use the center are between twenty-six and thirty-four, and a quarter are over fifty years. A large proportion appear to be homemakers who wish to work outside the home or train or retrain for an occupation. The services of the center have now been extended to men.

Education Information Centre. Brantford, a small city in the province of Ontario, has a population of approximately 69,000 and Brant County surrounding the city has another 29,000 people. No postsecondary institutions are located in Brantford, although three universities and a community college now offer varied courses locally, due in large part to the work of the Council on Continuing Education for Brantford and Brant County, which sponsors the Education Information Centre. Composed of both individual citizens and representatives of many education institutions, the council was set up in 1975; its first act was to open the Education Information Centre, which is administered by the council's executive director. While the centre is the council's main activity and visible agent in the community, the council's mandate extends to facilitating cooperative programs by educational institutions — identifying both overlaps and gaps in provision — promoting experimental projects, and performing a leadership/catalyst role locally to expand learning opportunities.

The Education Centre itself is situated in a large storefront in the main square in downtown Brantford. The director of the council spends a quarter of his time with center administration; most client counseling is conducted by his colleague. The secretary/receptionist handles most information and telephone queries and the information files, which contain material on a wide range of learning opportunities, local and national education, training employment, and labor market information. Other services include career and vocational planning, linking of skills, referrals, individual counseling, some outreach, and client advocacy when necessary. Eighty percent of clients walk in, women outnumber men two to one, and predominant age groups are twenty-three to twenty-five and over fifty. While all groups in the community use the center, a majority are of low to middle income. The council supports related projects, for example, a directory of local institutional resources and an energy conservation information center. These activities involve the center and the council in a community development milieu.

The Education Advice Centre. Cologne, the fourth largest city in the Federal Republic of Germany, houses the oldest counseling center for adults on the continent of Europe. With close to one million inhabitants, the city is now suffering from unemployment, most prevalent among the 100,000 foreign workers in the city. In 1976 the federal government launched experimental counseling centers for unemployed adults in ten communities. One of these special projects is administered by the Educational Advice Centres in Cologne.

Established in 1972, the center now has a large budget from the city with some project funds from the state and federal governments. Located on two floors in a small office building on a downtown shopping street, the center employs nineteen people. Its original services for schools and young people gradually broadened to include seminars for teachers and workers in social agencies, followed by the gradual introduction of counseling services for adults and for specialized "target" groups. For example, counseling is now offered to six inner-city schools in low-income areas with a concentration of unemployed workers and to foreign workers through small counseling units operating in several locations in the ethnic areas. These services are now primarily in the Turkish areas and are soon to be offered in Italian and Greek areas as well. An in-service training program has been developed by the senior counselor.

In the special project for the unemployed, women predominate. Yet men tend to predominate in the general adult counseling, perhaps because women's mobility has tended to diminish with the rise of economic uncertainty. The clients come from the upper group of the working class; the majority are twenty to thirty years old and motivated to engage in further education. In the foreign worker projects, males again predominate, perhaps because of cultural factors; these clients usually have a low educational level, are unaware of their civil rights, and tend to be subject to severe social and unemployment discrimination.

Educational Guidance Service for Adults (EGSA). Northern Ireland, with a population of over one and a half million, has an unemployment rate of over 11 percent. It has 27 institutions of further education and 150 out-centers providing vocational, academic, and recreational classes. It is served also by two universities, one polytechnic, the Open University, the Workers' Educational Association, and various government training centers, agricultural colleges, and other agencies.

Probably the oldest independent counseling service for adults still in existence, EGSA was set up in 1967 with a three-year grant from a charitable foundation. EGSA began under the aegis of the Northern Ireland Council for Social Service; the Association for Recurrent Education became a cosponsor in 1978. Its founders believed that independence and a community base would permit it to offer impartial advice and client advocacy without any conflicts of interest. EGSA has developed a strong network of colleagues and agencies, and client group and issue advocacy form an essential part of the service. From the beginning, EGSA maintained its independent basis, although it has suffered financial insecurity since 1974 and lost its entire government grant in 1978.

Located in offices in downtown Belfast, EGSA has one full-time organizer-counselor, aided by a secretary-receptionist and a part-time psychologist who administers tests. EGSA's services originally emphasized vocational guidance but have since broadened toward life planning and career and education counseling. The heart of the service is individual counseling; all interviews are by appointment and last an average of one hour, with several interviews per client being common. About one-third of the clients are tested and many clients return for follow-up sessions at regular intervals. Clients have numbered over 4,000 for the past twelve years, with an equal number of men and women and an age range from nineteen to over seventy, of which 50 percent are over twenty-five.

Model Differences

While these four centers have much in common in their philosophies, programs, and styles of operation, the differences that do exist seem either to flow from their structure—the "model" they have chosen to follow—or to reside in the unique activities that result from their program decisions. This section examines those characteristics of the models which seem to have influenced centers' existing services or which have the potential to do so in the future.

Institution-Based Model. The Women's Resources Center most closely resembles the institutional model, in which one education provider supplies a community-wide service. Many women's centers have grown out of institution-based programs. The strengths of its organic relationship with the University of British Columbia (UBC) include continuity of funding from one year to the next and the provision of institutional support for program priorities chosen by the WRC. The institutional link also helps WRC act as a programming source that can design specific programs for its clientele using university teachers and resources.

Weaknesses or dangers in one institution offering a community-wide service lie more in the perception that clients and the public may have of the service than in constraints imposed by the institution. WRC believes that because many women feel uncomfortable in a university-sponsored center, additional centers are needed to reach unserved target groups. No one center can help clients from every geographic area or socioeconomic background. Other educational institutions can feel threatened by what they may see as one institution's "promotional outreach" and therefore may be reluctant to cooperate with the center. Another danger is the temptation to give information more frequently about courses of the host institution and to counsel clients into those courses in preference to those of other institutions. Some institutions frankly admit that their counseling units are part of their recruitment apparatus; UBC does not and deliberately keeps WRC at arm's length in order to protect its neutrality. Because WRC does offer programs for UBC, however, clients in other institutions may view it as an "outlet" for one agency's offerings.

Perhaps a more serious weakness is the possibility of client and issue advocacy being restricted by an institution's sensitivity to the risks entailed by the advocate role. Often advocacy involves exerting pressure on government, public, or other education institutions, and group or issue advocacy in particular can cause publicity and hostility. The freedom of a center to engage in public advocacy or to press for policy changes may then be compromised by an institution's reluctance to engage in "political activity." The WRC appears to seek less overt ways of helping its clients than through open advocacy.

Community Council/Consortium Model. The Brantford Education Information Centre embraces aspects of both the community council and the consortium models. The members of the Council on Continuing Education include representatives of most of the educational institutions providing courses in the area, as well as lay members; all serve in a personal capacity as interested citizens. Some of the strengths of the broad base of support are obvious; the involvement of institutional providers and individual citizens in a cooperative undertaking releases much community energy that can be directed toward improving local access to learning opportunities. The promotion of such a center, particularly in a small community under 100,000 people, becomes a function of having many key leaders on the board; such members constitute a powerful referral network that both clients and staff can use. Promoting a client-centered image becomes much easier with a broad sponsor base because the center is less likely to be perceived as a feeder for any one institution. Advocacy, particularly at the client level, is a more accepted task of such a center. In Brantford's case, issue and group advocacy are a function of the council itself, which it performs with vigor. This two-step advocacy, in which the center handles client matters and the council takes up the issues, seems possible only when a counseling center's government has both a broad membership and a philosophy oriented toward innovation. A consortium of providers only would be unlikely to take on issue advocacy, but, if joined together with lay members in a community council, it might be able to weather the public controversy that advocacy often stimulates.

The major weakness frequently found in these services based on community councils or consortia is a lack of financial security because no one agency takes full responsibility for the service. Although a good council may have good access to the local governments, it must compete annually for its budget with many other community needs; state grants that may give greater security often are on a project or short-term basis only. The pure consortium model may tend to stifle innovative or alternative forms of continuing education if these are perceived as a threat to the established providers, while the lay council model, which lacks the strength of the institutions, may not have the will or the credibility to undertake risky ventures. A mix of council and consortium models could render a center especially vulnerable because the providers must share the responsibility for the center with its lay members. Yet in Brantford, the mix of the community council and consortium models seems to have avoided the weaknesses and created a hybrid that has stimulated experiments and change.

Local Government Model. The Cologne Centre exhibits a very unusual organizing principle, the local government-sponsored service. The detailed plans for the center that the director drew up in the early seventies may account for the center's success in securing support monies from the city and special project funds from state and federal governments. Cologne appears to be the only municipal government that fully funds an educational counseling service. The center does serve young people as well as adults; the career counseling offered to students before they enter the labor market and the special projects to serve foreign workers and the unemployed may indicate the priority that the city and the staff assign to its practical orientation. The security and continuity of its funding may result from being a recognized municipal unit offering a valued service. Its clientele appears to view it as just another local service open to all because it is provided by the government. Being located apart from city hall and administered at arm's length as a special unit also may help the center maintain its client-centered independence.

The weaknesses of the model, like its strengths, are hard to illustrate because there are so few examples. Client or group advocacy, or pressure for changes in public policy affecting education, could be difficult to undertake in a government-sponsored service. Yet this center has been successful in mediating between some individuals and educational institutions and has exercised leadership by recommending to government and to institutions many new policies to correct unjust practices and to combat educational deficits and social dysfunctions. While the center sees itself as a proactive agent in recommending legislative changes and in case advocacy, it may be that advocacy has a different connotation in Germany, with its highly structured, integrated, and sequentially organized education system. Until more communities adopt this model for a counseling service for adult learners, a weakness relating to advocacy is difficult to prove.

Brokerage Model. The Belfast Educational Guidance Service for Adults is an independent education broker. Similar to the classic education brokerages that have swept across the United States since the middle seventies, EGSA probably pioneered the concept of the autonomous community-based service that is both fiscally and organizationally independent and self-directing. Founded ten years before the term "educational brokering" was coined, the Belfast center has exhibited the major strengths and weaknesss of this model over its thirteen years of life. The strengths reside mainly in its independence of all providers, in the perception of clients and providers alike of the impartial nature of its information and advice, and in its powerful image of client advocate. Derived mainly from the freestanding nature of the organization, this image may have been enhanced by EGSA's continuity of staffing (the original director still guides the service). Its independent status allows case and group advocacy to operate effectively and facilitates policy interventions with both institutions and governments. Advocacy is made easier, too, by the close links that EGSA established with agencies and individuals in order to provide a service from a community base. Those links have been forged over the years into a potent and influential network.

Perhaps the only serious weakness in this model is that its independent, community-rooted nature has left EGSA vulnerable financially. All independent brokerages have had funding difficulties; most have set up shop with government grants given for the short term or for demonstrations. Some experiment with client fees or contracts for consultation services; others spend resources looking for special project grants, which deflects them from their main purpose. Probably the most negative aspect is the insecurity engendered by uncertain funding, which debilitates staff and discourages supporters. EGSA has suffered financial uncertainty for some years; hopes for a permanent government grant have not yet been realized. One other potential weakness in this model may be the nominal rather than real cooperation from the providers. The other models carry some commitment from one or more institutions to give financial or moral support to the counseling function; the independent broker, on the other hand, has to win support by demonstrating that the rewards from its service to learners will accrue indirectly to the providers. EGSA tried to counter this danger by nourishing its network through the years. Promoting the work of an independent center, however, will always be a continuing task requiring energy and persistence.

Models to Transplant

Three important and innovative aspects of the centers studied do seem to be fairly independent of the administrative structure and may be transportable to other situations and communities. First, the use of volunteers as peer counselors, so successfully demonstrated in the Vancouver center, could be adopted in the other models with no difficulty, provided that a suitable orientation program were also introduced. Fostering a cadre of trained volunteers would be a natural way for centers to reach more clients with more services. Peer counselors can facilitate clients' movement toward autonomy, since they are models of self-directed learners themselves. Volunteers, too, can initiate outreach and development activities, thereby enlarging centers' catchment areas and stimulating replication of services to other target populations.

Second, the lack of educational standards for counselors of adults and of suitable educational materials has hampered many agencies. The Cologne Centre reported a great need for both as it attempted to design a quality in-service education sequence. In addition to the Vancouver volunteer education program, useful instructional materials should result from the special project in which Syracuse University and the National Center for Educational Brokering (1979) are developing new models and procedures to select and train counselors. All educational modules will be designed for use by existing staffs to develop new areas of expertise as well as helping professionals and volunteers entering counseling to acquire technical and information skills to strengthen their referral capabilities.

Third, all centers demonstrated some proficiency in group and issue advocacy; this area, however, does seem less free of contamination by certain factors inherent in the chosen model. In the Regional Learning Service study (Riffer, 1978), the investigators sought to discover the ways in which a broker could be effective in advocating for adult learners as a group. After RLS surveyed adult students and identified existing and perceived barriers to adult learners, it concluded that certain conditions must exist for a brokerage to facilitate change. If the collaborative mode of relating to institutions is not successful, a broker may have to adopt an adversary relationship with the provider, for example, by organizing adult students as consumers or using the media to attract attention to learners' problems. RLS also predicted that efforts at the system level to get institutional policies changed or new legislation established were likely to increase substantially in the future. So while some models seem to facilitate case and issue advocacy more than others, no serious impediments exist to any center increasing its efforts to improve access to learning opportunities for its adult clients through group advocacy. Lacking vested interests in providing instruction or attracting students, counseling centers may serve learners best by working in this unique way to enhance the learning environment in their communities.

None of the models found in the literature or discussed here is perfect. An analysis of the needs of a particular situation or community must always be undertaken before a particular form or structure is adopted. Yet one should remember that a supportive environment can foster an effective learner-centered counseling service. If staff energy must be directed constantly to seeking financial stability, full attention cannot be given to serving clients; if administrators are nervous about an advocacy stance, the center's freedom to lobby for improving access to learning will be compromised.

Yet success cannot be guaranteed by form. In some cases, the desire to be learner-oriented or to offer impartial advice may override a barrier or another inhibiting aspect of a particular structure. All four centers, in fact, shared to a marked degree three characteristics that could be called "ideal elements." The most important, a distinct orientation to learners' needs, infused centers' philosophy of service and their actual programs, even of those centers sponsored by one institution or government. The other ideal elements exhibited by all centers were an emphasis on the primary purpose for which the center was established and strong links with the community through an outreach or referral network. Since these characteristics depend heavily on the people involved, one might conclude that vigorous leadership and commitment to the primacy of facilitating learning have the power to override many functional constraints.

References

Advisory Council for Adult and Continuing Education. *Links to Learning*. Leicester, U.K.: Advisory Council for Adult and Continuing Education, 1979.

Clyne, P. *Adult Education for Underprivileged Groups*. DESC-EE S (79) 48. Strasbourg: Council for Cultural Cooperation, Council of Europe, 1979.

Ironside, D. J. "Innovations in Counselling of and Information-Giving to Adult Learners in North America." *International Journal for the Advancement of Counselling*, 1979, *3*, 199–211.

Ironside, D. J. *Models for Counselling Adult Learners: Four Case Studies*. Toronto: Ontario Institute for Studies in Education, 1980.

National Center for Educational Brokering. "The NCEB-S.U. Project Selecting and Training Adult Counsellors." *National Center for Educational Brokering Bulletin*, 1979, *4* (8), 1–3.

17

Paltridge, J. G., Regan, M. C., and Terkla, D. G. *Mid-Career Education and Training; Community Support Systems: California Studies in Community Policy and Change,* no. 6. Davis: Institute of Governmental Affairs, University of California, 1979.

Riffer, N. W. "The CEIC Project." *National Center for Educational Brokering Bulletin,* 1978, *3* (9), 1-3.

Diana J. Ironside is chairperson of the Departmental Admissions Committee and professor of adult education in the Ontario Institute for Studies in Education. She is also president of the Canadian Congress of Learning Opportunities for Older Women.

Workplace counselors increase access to myriad opportunities that are essential if workers are to cope with the increasing complexities of work and personal life.

Workplace Counseling: The Missing Link

Herbert A. Levine
Deborah Hanwell Piggins

A husband and wife earning a combined income of $38,000 as factory workers lose their jobs in a plant closing. Neither speaks English. Neither has gone beyond the ninth grade. Neither has a marketable skill.

A recently widowed woman needs skill upgrading to advance so that she can support her two children, but her job is in jeopardy because of her erratic attendance.

A young man with a growing family thinks he may be able to advance with additional education, but his past experience with education has been so negative that he is afraid of returning to the classroom.

These are the kinds of people who usually fall through the cracks in the educational system. Past the age of "traditional" students, they have no readily available guide to point them toward appropriate resources.

The United States has demonstrated its belief in the need for education until age sixteen, but has largely ignored the desperate need of adult workers to pursue various kinds of education and training. With information the fastest-growing industry in the world, technological change burgeoning everywhere, and economics and politics growing ever more complex, the need for all workers to have lifelong access to information, training, and education becomes urgent. The need is especially great for those at the low end of the economic and employment ladder: people without marketable skills, and without basic literacy. Nationwide surveys have indicated that the "lack of basic skills in reading and computation may be one of the major barriers associated with structural or chronic unemployment" (Williams, 1980, p. 10). Accepting these needs as a given, the next logical step is to provide adult workers with a means of access to educational opportunities. One workable vehicle for doing this is a system of educational advisement and counseling connected directly with the workplace.

Current Programs

Labor unions have long been interested in providing such opportunities for members and their families and to that end have negotiated such vehicles as tuition refund, release time, and special programs. For instance, the United Auto Workers (UAW) contracts provide for a refund of $1,000 per member per year, and the International Union of Electrical, Radio, and Machine Workers specifies $800. Many have also developed unilateral educational programs and funds to meet the particular needs of their membership, including apprenticeship training, leadership and other labor education subjects, and health and safety. Some unions, like the International Union of Operating Engineers and the International Brotherhood of Electrical Workers (IBEW), are combining their apprenticeship programs with associate degrees through cooperation with community colleges, as in the Tripartite Program for Apprenticeship and Associate Degree in Labor Studies, coordinated by the George Meany Labor Studies Center (Hindle, 1980). Some unions have comprehensive, union-run educational facilities. The IBEW provides everything from opera to basic literacy at its Long Island education and cultural center, Bayberryland, financed jointly with contractors who contribute .5 percent of the payroll. The UAW maintains year-round programs in labor education, general education, and training at its Walter and May Reuther Family Education Center at Black Lake, Michigan, which is financed by dues. In New York, District Council 37 of the American Federation of State, County, and Municipal Workers has been a leader in educational innovations. It has developed a highly successful college degree program at its own headquarters with the College of New Rochelle. In conjunction with Local 1199 of the Health and Hospital Workers and with funds from the City of New York, it offers members in the health industry up to two and a half years of educational leave at 80 percent of salary for professional improvement.

Employers also provide extensive educational opportunities for their employees, including on-the-job training, skill upgrading, management skills, and other job-related programs. Traditionally, these programs are geared for managerial, technical, and white-collar workers and tend to be job-specific. Larger companies have tuition reimbursement plans for individual development. Tuition refund programs are widespread in large American companies, although only about 3 percent of those eligible seem to participate in these opportunities. Some companies, however, such as Kimberly-Clark, provide for individual educational pursuits through a cumulative educational fund supported by contributions from the company and the employee; they have achieved employee participation rates as high as 48 percent.

Principal among the opportunities offered to the unemployed is the multifaceted Comprehensive Employment and Training Act (CETA) system. Its various education and training programs, run in conjunction with labor, industry, and the educational system, specifically aim toward providing employment by improving skills. There are also public funds for individual educational pursuits of the unemployed or disadvantaged, including the Basic Educational Opportunity Grant, and the Tuition Assistance Program. In addition, many state governments provide services in English as a Second Language (ESL), General Education Diploma (GED), and basic literacy for a nominal registration fee.

Barriers

One might begin to think that with so many educational programs available to the adult worker there would be little room for improvement. But statistics paint a gloomy picture of increasing illiteracy in the population as a whole, a considerable number of immigrants who neither speak nor understand English, and a serious problem of vocational illiteracy. Yet with the obvious need for adult worker education, study after study (Botsman, 1975; Charnèr and others, 1978; Levine and Cohen-Rosenthal, 1977) has found the existing opportunities to be barely touched. Those same studies identify a consistent pattern of institutional and psychic barriers including:

1. *Lack of information.* Few workers know what is available to them and how to get it.
2. *Lack of money.* Even where there is a tuition refund plan, workers do not have enough ready cash to pay tuition and wait months for reimbursement.
3. *Family disruptions.* Time spent in class and studying is time away from the family. This is hard on any worker but is especially difficult for women, single parents, and those who cannot afford babysitters. When an adult goes to school, it affects the whole family.
4. *Fear.* The adults most in need of access to education are those who have been most damaged by earlier experiences with institutions. Nearly every adult student must deal with fear of failure.
5. *Restrictions of the refund.* Tuition refund programs are often very restrictive. The terms of the refund may stipulate job-related or degree courses.
6. *Institutional insensitivity.* The would-be adult student is not unaware that the educational system has ignored the needs and aspirations of the average worker. Problems of poor scheduling, lack of outreach, lack of innovative approaches to teaching and delivery, and lack of support services all contribute to the chasm dividing workers from the educational system.

It becomes clear that overcoming the barriers to worker participation in education is a complex undertaking that will require cooperation and planning among labor, industry, government, and education.

Enter the Workplace Counselor

In light of the adult worker's educational and personal needs and barriers, it becomes important to provide counseling assistance. A discussion of effective assistance would focus on the individual counselor, the counseling process, and the importance of union commitment.

The Person. One of the interesting sidelights turned up by various studies of adult workers is that those who have overcome the barriers and have had some educational success become hooked and are natural advocates for worker education. Often these same people rise through the ranks to become committee people, stewards, representatives, officers. Here is an untapped resource that could provide a core of workplace counselors. The workplace counselor is not a professional in the sense of a social worker or psychologist, but rather a specially trained peer counselor. The counselor should bring to his or her work certain qualities such as experience with bumping heads with the barriers of the system; a nonjudgmental attitude about people and their problems; a positive attitude toward problem solving that will enable him or her to bring together needs and resources; and a basic integrity that will encourage the trust and confidence of the individual worker, the union, the institution, and the employer. Building on those personal qualities, the counselor needs knowledge of counseling techniques; structure and function of the systems he will deal with (union, employer, education, political, support services); information and public relations; communications and self-presentation skills; and the identification and use of various resources.

The Counseling Process. Once oriented, the workplace counselor becomes involved in what is basically a three-step process. The first step is for the counselor to inform other workers of what opportunities are available, how to take advantage of them, and how the counselor can help. This may be accomplished by speaking at meetings of officers, stewards, or rank-and-file members; writing articles for the union newspaper; posting flyers and notices on bulletin boards; spreading the word person-to-person; and many other ways.

When an individual decides to make use of the counselor, the second step of the process begins. The counselor must first help the worker identify and assess his own proficiencies. Then the worker needs to identify a short-term goal; this is related to the worker's reason for consulting the counselor. Does he want to go back to school for personal enrichment or job advancement or to gain basic literacy skills or change careers? Once this immediate goal is known, the counselor may think it necessary to find out the worker's level. It may be advisable to have aptitude or interest testing. Or the peer counselor may become aware of a personal problem that requires referral of the worker to a professional. If a goal appears to be unrealistic for the individual worker, the counselor needs to be able to demonstrate through assessment, offering reasonable alternatives and without destroying the worker's confidence, that the goal may be unreachable. However, the counselor cannot make that decision for the worker.

If the worker decides to pursue his goal, the counselor then provides him with information about all the alternative methods of reaching that goal. It is the worker who decides which method is best for him. The counselor and worker then develop a plan of action that will guide what part each will play. For instance, in the beginning the worker may feel that he needs extra help and moral support from the counselor. As he gains confidence, this may change and he may want to use the counselor only as a source of information or to make new contacts. The counselor must know when to offer a hand without being paternalistic and how to be helpful without making the worker over-dependent on him.

In another situation, a worker may go to the counselor with the knowledge that he is going to be laid off and with absolutely no idea what he wants to do or is capable of or what is available. In that case, the most practical first step is for the counselor to consult various economic and job forecasts as to what fields are growing and where the jobs will be, while referring the worker for assessment of interest and aptitude. When the worker considers the results of this combined effort, he should be able to make a reasonably well-informed decision about what direction he wants to take.

The third and last step for the workplace counselor is to establish linkages with the various institutions and agencies that will serve the worker/student. This often involves the creation of innovative and flexible programs and delivery systems. It also includes organizing group learning activities. One of the most valuable things a workplace counselor can do is to develop networks of information and services, to get people talking to each other about what they can do for each other. For instance, if an educational institution with declining enrollment were aware that a local union had a tuition refund arrangement, it might be very willing to develop some innovative programs for the membership and deliver them on-site.

The whole process entails the counselor identifying options and providing information and the worker making informed decisions. The counselor is not a decision maker. He can give the client a map and tell him about the potholes and speed traps and the rules of the road, but the worker must choose the route and drive the car.

The Link with the Union. In many cases, a worker's commitment to education is a long-term one. It is therefore important that the workplace counselor be a recognized part of an organization that has a long-term commitment to worker education. Since labor unions have advocated and provided worker education from their inception, they are the natural environment for the workplace counselor. Many unions already offer their members social service or family counseling. The workplace counselor might work full-time doing educational counseling or part-time as a regular employee and part-time as a counselor on the union staff. It is important for the sake of the workers' trust in the counselor that the counselor be a part of the organization that represents the worker. The counselor, like a good shop steward, must deal with the whole person and all the possible problems that might affect his education or work. A worker would be hesitant to discuss many of those problems with a representative of the employer. The counselor, while advocating for the worker, can be a creative problem solver in working out more cooperation among union, management, and educators to provide better educational opportunities. The workplace counselor should not be attached to a particular institution or recruit for any one institution.

While it is important that educational institutions have counselors who understand and can deal with problems of the worker/student, those counselors do not replace the workplace counselors. The two should complement each other in serving the worker, since one knows the intricacies of a particular institution and the other is more familiar with the worker as a whole person in his work and home environments. The workplace counselor should be able to move easily through the systems of industry, education, government, labor, and the community to form networks and solve problems in a constructive manner, but he should understand that he is an advocate for the education of workers to better their work and personal lives.

The Counselor at Work

Although the concept of advocating worker education and providing advising, counseling, and learning in the workplace has gained some acceptance in Europe, most notably in Sweden, it is still in the experimental stages in the United States.

The publications of the National Center for Educational Brokering and the Worker Education and Training Project of the National Institute for Work and Learning attest to the fact that many organizations and institutions are trying to respond to the needs of adult learners. At the Rutgers University Labor Education Center, the Occupational Advancement Project is training CETA participants to work as education advisers with unions and community-based organizations.

Perhaps the counseling relationship is best illustrated by describing the three cases mentioned at the beginning of this chapter. None of these counseling relationships has been concluded yet, but they are representative of the multifaceted and often ongoing nature of workplace counseling.

In the first case, the counselor was working with a foreign-born couple who had never learned English. Although they were members of a union that provided tuition refunds, they did not know about the program until a workplace counselor was assigned to work with them shortly after they had been laid off.

Their comfortable income and sense of security on the job had insulated them from many problems associated with language barriers and lack of marketable skills. Suddenly they were confronted with unemployment and no knowledge of what the system might offer them. In their first meeting with the counselor, they decided that because their jobs had been eliminated by foreign trade, they were eligible for TRA (Trade Readjustment) benefits. That, added to their unemployment benefits, would give them a modest income for one year. The man, however, was adamant about getting a job and said he would like to learn truck driving and get a GED. The woman had no particular career interest beyond earning a living but wanted to get her GED in Spanish. The counselor suggested that they visit the Adult Learning Center to begin the process of enrolling and to have some assessment of their educational levels and needs. Because the two were nervous about school and testing, the counselor went with them and introduced them to the bilingual counselor, the registrar, and a GED instructor.

Between the first and second meetings, the counselor determined that there was no truck-driving school in the area that was approved for TRA-funded training. He found out through a labor colleague that a union specializing in heavy equipment operation had openings in its apprenticeship program, but when the counselor called a union official, he learned that applicants needed a high school diploma or GED. The union official referred the counselor to one of their industrial units that was hiring and would do on-the-job training without a high school diploma. When the counselor called the company's personnel department, he learned that the training was given only in English.

The counselor presented this information to the couple for their consideration, along with the news that the man might be able to get a job in another plant that the union represented. The assessment from the Learning Center indicated that both needed a beginning ESL course, tutoring in math, and American history. The counselor informed the couple that they also had the option of enrolling in ESL at the local community college, and that if they continued as students and accumulated twenty-four credits, they would receive high school diplomas automatically. Both decided to take ESL together, and the man opted for the GED in Spanish as the shortest route. Because he was also anxious to go back to work, the counselor referred the man to the appropriate union officials, who made the necessary arrangements with the other plant. The woman preferred not to go back to full-time work until she had a good grasp of English.

In order to take the ESL course together, the couple needed childcare for their two youngsters. The counselor assisted them in finding reputable childcare facilities and babysitters, which, unfortunately, were not provided by the Learning Center. The counselor continued to speak with them periodically as they progressed, ready to give additional information when necessary. As they approach their initial goals, he will discuss with them their next steps to a stable employment future.

In the second case, a female worker was referred to the counselor by the union president. She was interested in some additional education so she could bid for a better-paying job but had already received a written reprimand from personnel for absence and lateness. At the first meeting, the counselor learned that she was recently widowed and needed a larger income to support her two children. The counselor suspected that the worker's attendance problem might be connected with alcohol, so he spoke with the union president, shop steward, and department head, who all had the same impression. When approached by her supervisor, the woman agreed to accept alcohol abuse counseling, and the workplace counselor referred her to a Certified Alcohol Counselor. When the workplace counselor and the woman met again, she revealed that she had a retarded child at home and was quite distraught because she did not feel capable of dealing with him all alone. She had neither the inclination nor the finances to institutionalize him. The counselor recognized this as a potentially serious problem and recommended that the woman discuss it with her alcohol abuse counselor so that they could deal with it and tap other social service resources if necessary.

Because both the counselor and the worker agreed that lack of money was a major problem and contributed to the others, the woman decided to go ahead with her educational plans while she tried to cope with everything else. The counselor was able to provide her with the name of a part-time special education teacher who did babysitting at night. There was neither released time for educational activities nor tuition refund available. The woman's only route for upgrading in her work situation seemed to be through civil service testing, for which she would need some preparation. The counselor found several other people who were interested in civil service preparation, and is now working with the local union president and an adult school to develop a course at the union headquarters immediately after work.

The case of the young man who wanted to advance is less complicated but more typical of problems encountered by counselors. He had been a marginal student who did not like school or get along with most teachers. At his parents' insistence, he had attended one term at a community college but had dropped out with lower than average grades and vowed never to return. After doing routine maintenance work for several years, he decided he was neither satisfied nor making ends meet very well.

A workplace counselor contacted him in response to his answers on a needs assessment survey, which indicated that he was interested in career change. It was clear to the counselor that this man was terrified of tests, so at first she referred him for a preference test only. The man was somewhat reassured by the nonthreatening nature of the test and was pleased when he showed a strong preference for social service and health work. Using her *Dictionary of Occupational Titles* and *Occupational Outlook Handbook,* the counselor identified several types of jobs that seemed to have good futures in health services and then suggested sources where the worker could get more details about what was involved in each job.

There were a few problems that the two had to solve: Tuition refund was limited to job-related courses, the man still had a strong hostility toward tests and teachers, and the man's wife was not altogether happy about the prospect of having to stay home with the children two nights a week and give up weekends as well while he studied. The employer refused to bend on the tuition refund regulations, but it turned out that the worker was still eligible for his GI education benefits. In order to help the worker overcome his fears and to get his wife involved in the whole process, the counselor arranged to spend a day with them at the community college where the man was thinking of applying. She set up appointments with a counselor there, who arranged to include in the meeting some other adult students, two instructors, and the director of the women's center. The day was a success. The man was relieved to find that "teachers had changed" since he was young and the woman was pleased to be a part of the planning. She even decided to take one of the free daytime minicourses offered by the women's center, which included free childcare on the premises. The man is now in his first term as a part-time student.

Where Do We Go from Here?

These cases illustrate ways to increase access to education; they also show the serious shortcomings of a system that has too many inflexibilities. Improving worker access to education is not a job that can or should be done by one organization. It is an enormous undertaking that should involve the cooperation and participation of labor, management, government, and the educational system. There are a number of recommendations to substantially improve worker participation in education.

First, the opportunities now available need to be expanded and improved. Stipulations for use of tuition refund need to be broadly defined to include more than job-related education or courses leading to degrees. More released time and paid leave for educational pursuits are needed.

Second, even good vehicles for increased access are useless if the educational system is unresponsive. Educators accustomed to dealing with traditional students need to change some of their preconceived stereotypes of workers and develop flexible delivery systems, schedules, and support systems like childcare.

Finally, very little will change without a concerted, cooperative effort to create national policy, laws, and appropriations for adult learning projects. There needs to be a national body as well as regional bodies made up of government, labor, industry, education, and community representatives that can help to create policy, exchange information, and begin to do some intelligent and realistic planning about how to provide lifelong learning opportunities for workers to create a more dynamic work force and a more informed populace.

Federal and state governments should appropriate monies to be used by various organizations and agencies, including labor unions, in providing educational opportunities to adult workers. The creation of a federally funded Labor Education Institute to coordinate research and action for worker educa-

28

tion would be a positive step in that direction. For too long, most participants in the educational structure have tried to ignore labor or have gone to the other extreme of trying to tell unions and their members what kind of education they need. Unions must be recognized as a source of knowledge and expertise in many areas and as rightful partners in the educational system.

References

Botsman, P. *The Learning Needs and Interests of Adult Blue-Collar Factory Workers.* An Extension Publication. Ithaca, N.Y.: New York State College of Human Ecology, Cornell University, 1975.

Charner, I., and others. *An Untapped Resource: Negotiated Tuition-Aid in the Private Sector.* Washington, D.C.: National Manpower Institute, 1978.

Hindle, R. Z., and others. *Tripartite Program for Apprenticeship and Associate Degree in Labor Studies.* Silver Springs, Md.: George Meany Center for Labor Studies, 1980.

Levine, H. A., and Cohen-Rosenthal, E. *Promising Horizons: Cooperative Opportunities Among Labor, Management, Education, and CETA in New Jersey.* New Brunswick, N.J.: Rutgers University, 1977.

Williams, E. B., and others. *Governor's Task Force on Unemployment in Atlantic City.* Final report. Trenton: State of New Jersey, 1980.

Herbert A. Levine is director of the Labor Education Center at Rutgers University and a consultant on tuition aid program and worker education.

Deborah Hanwell Piggins is director of the Occupational Advancement Project at the Rutgers Labor Education Center.

Working adults retain more of what they learn when learning is self-directed. Counselors help employees over the hurdle as they choose individualized learning experiences.

In the Private Sector, There Is a Choice

Bart L. Ludeman

Within the past decade, we have experienced an unprecedented increase in laws, regulations, and public demand concerning the freedom and right of people to learn. Coupled with that, private sector management has become aware that productivity and employee loyalty are declining while turnover and absenteeism are on the upswing. Management's concern is to make human effort and energy count.

Employers can no longer legally require courses or degrees in given positions, unless they can validate the need for them. At the same time, there is pressure on management to provide quality learning experiences for employees in the work setting.

Career counselors in business and industry hope to satisfy individual needs. But their major goal is to find ways to develop productive and satisfied employees. Their job is to gain agreement among management, employee, and supervisor and to help develop a contract with the employee in concert with corporate goals.

Lloyds Bank California is relatively small among the major banks, but dedicated to developing individual careers and placing employees in positions that can best utilize their talents. Each employee is counseled twice each year. The counselor helps them review their goals and assess their willingness to spend the necessary time and effort to develop their career and to take the risks involved in learning and growing.

Documented career counseling is part of the regular review process. At that time, the manager is expected to outline employee strengths and drawbacks and to recognize and review further potential. Each employee sees an overview of all positions within the bank and the requirements necessary to attain them. He completes a "Position Preference Checklist" and is given an opportunity to write a "Learning Contract" to formulate learning objectives and sort out career goal priorities.

The Position Preference Checklist allows employees to check their position and indicate their level of satisfaction with that position. This information is used along with the annual performance review to allow the bank to properly assess the goals and career objectives of employees. The Learning Contract is utilized after the career counseling session where the learning needs for improvement and growth were identified, and where career opportunities were mutually agreed upon. The Learning Contract specifies the "self-directed" learning needed, how to carry out the learning, how to know when it has been accomplished, who could verify the accomplishments, and how they would be verified. Thus, the Learning Contract makes visible the mutual responsibilities of the employee and the bank.

Professionalism and objectivity are stressed in the second counseling session, which takes place midway through the year. The counselors are assistant managers of the units, who have been thoroughly trained in counseling and career planning techniques as a part of their development. In addition, counselors are taught to use resources such as local colleges and universities, consultants, coaches, libraries, and competing businesses to advise employees of the learning avenues available.

The Assessment Process

If employees aspire to management positions, it is recommended that they become participants in the Assessment Center. Here, management and sales abilities are assessed and activities are designed to enhance strengths and reduce weaknesses. The employee receives counseling from a personnel professional in the presence of the manager. Again, it is recommended that a learning contract be designed as part of the employee's overall self-directed learning. This portion of the contract is followed by the personnel officer, and the education officer and manager are kept informed.

The Learning Contract

While Malcolm Knowles' concept of self-directed learning (1975) has been successful in many institutions of higher education, it is not yet widely used in the private sector. The approach is appealing to both management and employee because it requires a "contract" with binding agreements on the part of both parties. The employee agrees to avenues to enhance proficiencies. The manager agrees that, when evidence is shown, the employee's improved performance will be recognized and rewarded.

Learning contracts are new to many. The education officer must use professional skills in explaining the concept and in getting the employee over the hurdle of making a choice toward self-directed education. When supervisors specify what employees must do to improve their proficiencies, the results are often poor because the employees have not participated in the decisions.

More recently, professional counselors in the personnel division have designed guidebooks and career counseling worksheets that are available as a resource to the education officer and are also open to the employee. As the contract is formed, the employee's manager is again included in learning negotiations. A similar process is available to every employee at every level.

Learning Strategies—The Choice

While employees are consistently encouraged to develop their own contracts, as an integral part of the counseling process education officers and personnel officers also suggest needed educational development. Many avenues of development are reviewed by the education officer, and employees choose those which best fit their individual needs. These avenues are as follows:

1. *Degrees, Certificates, Courses.* California is noted for a college and university system that addresses the needs of employers within communities. Bank employees are encouraged to take courses related to work and to future goals. Three years ago, fewer than 5 percent took advantage of this opportunity, but with the advent of self-directed learning the number has increased to 35 percent. Many work toward cooperative education credit and full degrees. The employee begins with an eye toward learning to enhance proficiencies and progress within the corporation. Because the higher education system places so much emphasis on credit, the student soon believes a degree or certificate program will be more meaningful to the employer. For years, the corporation has placed emphasis on in-company training programs and in many cases has validated their effectiveness on the job. The employee believes this training should be integrated into the degree program and wants full credit.

2. *Coaching and Counseling.* With the learning contract comes a need to identify managers and technicians within the corporation who can provide learning experiences to the novice. Many employees choose a coach or mentor who monitors progress, points to strengths and weaknesses in performance, and provides guidance within a real-world environment. This mode is particularly helpful in developing management and sales proficiencies and receives a positive acceptance from managers. Coupled with formal education, this is the second most popular choice by employees.

3. *Continuing Education.* Continuing education offices on college and university campuses provide significant help in facilitating self-directed study. They are particularly helpful in the development of second careers, a growing phenomenon that is still difficult for managers in the private sector to accept. The counselor's role can be a significant one for the educator if he or she has an understanding of the world of work. The employee also tends to favor public seminars and workshops as well as counseling provided by the continuing

education office. A high number of instructors are hired from the business sector, which brings real-world values to the student. Business and industry see such education as a greater return on their investment because what is learned in such classrooms can be applied more directly to the job.

4. *Volunteer/Professional Groups.* While a great deal of learning takes place outside formal educational or work settings, it is difficult to measure. If employees can apply knowledge from such informal continuing education to their work, proficiencies are enhanced. Learning need not be formally structured to take place. This is especially true in the development of interpersonal effectiveness.

5. *Reading and Audio Visuals.* Many employees seek avenues that allow individual learning. Under the umbrella of self-directed learning, more and more home study programs have been developed. Currently, employees can find books, cassette tapes, slides, and films on almost any subject. Closed-circuit videotape has allowed us to make great strides in educational development, and with the advent of Betamax and other modes, we will see a marked increase in home study programs.

Conclusion

The use of multiple counseling techniques and learning contracts in career development is a step forward in private sector counseling. It is a comprehensive effort that takes into account the dynamic interdependence of the multiple elements that comprise every organization and every individual. New employee values and attitudes continue to emerge; people want something more than symbols of conventional success.

The target of the eighties is increased productivity. Worker competence and fulfillment in the workplace has a major influence on the productivity profile. While self-directed development and creative counseling are not the only avenues, they are central.

We need to continue to move ahead with new concepts in counseling, take advantage of the vast resources for development, and remember that quality work life encourages employees to make decisions for themselves. It gives them a choice of where they are going and of how to get there.

Reference

Knowles, M. *Self-Directed Learning.* Chicago: Association Press, 1975.

Bart L. Ludeman is a consultant in human resources development and a former vice-president and director of human resources development at Lloyds Bank California. In 1978 he was the national president of the American Society for Training and Development. He is also active in the American Association of Community and Junior Colleges, the Califiornia Cooperative Education Association, and the International Assessment Center Congress.

The Reentry Adult Student Project offers a model for examining the needs and satisfactions of adult students in two-year colleges.

Easing Academic Reentry

Joseph A. Mangano
Thomas J. Corrado

Academic reentry can be a harrowing experience for adult students. Returning to formal education after an absence of more than five years, adults over twenty-five have little knowledge of academic life and are easily overwhelmed by its demands. They tend to view college as an alien environment in which administrative policies, instructional practices, support services, language, and even attitudes are typically tailored to the needs of younger students (McDermott, 1975). Moreover, many reentry adult students:

- are handicapped by communication deficiences, poor study skills, and low self-confidence
- are constrained by family and job responsibilities that interfere with their academic pursuits
- are easily frustrated by institutional "red tape"
- are highly motivated but anxious about their ability to compete with younger, "sharper" students
- are hampered by misinformation concerning intelligence, learning, and memory.

Given these impediments to educational progress, it is not surprising that a substantial number of adults reentering academic programs experience apprehension, disorientation, and failure.

The challenge created by the current mixing of generations in the classroom demands a commitment to lifelong learning through which postsecondary institutions recast their efforts to integrate adult students into the campus communities.

The Reentry Adult Student Project

In response to this challenge, in 1977 the Two-Year College Development Center of the State University of New York at Albany, with support from the New York State Education Department, initiated the Reentry Adult Student Project (RASP). The objectives of this project were to examine the needs and satisfactions of adult students in New York State two-year colleges and to assist those colleges in providing programs and support services for adult students (Mangano and Corrado, 1979).

From the pool of fifty-seven two-year colleges in New York State with eligibility to receive vocational education funding, six representative colleges were selected as pilot sites. The president of each college appointed a steering committee to serve as liaison between the college and the center in coordinating local participation. The steering committees comprised various administrative and faculty representatives, and included deans of continuing education, deans of instruction, deans of students, directors of institutional research, department chairs, faculty members, counselors, and reentry adult students. They were charged with developing a local work plan, surveying selected campus groups, disseminating project findings to the campus community, and recommending implementation activities at the local level.

At each college, selected samples of traditional college students (N = 561) (up to twenty-four years of age), reentry adult students (N = 529) (twenty-five years and older), and faculty and staff (N = 199) were surveyed during the 1978–79 academic year using two questionnaires designed by the project staff: the Survey of Student Needs and the Student Satisfaction Scale. The traditional college students were typically single, matriculated, full-time students enrolled in day classes, and had a break of one year or less in formal education. In contrast to this group, over two-thirds of the reentry adults were part-time students, employed, married, attending evening classes, with a lapse of five years or more in formal education.

Student Needs Assessment. In this component of RASP, the responses of the groups to each item of the Survey of Student Needs were compared using the chi-square statistic.

Twelve of the fifty-one items that statistically differentiated the younger and older students were given higher ratings (indicating greater perceived need) by the adults. These twelve items included vocabulary and math skill improvement; lecture classes; independent study courses; evening, weekend, and summer classes and registration; life experience credit; three-hour classes; preregistration opportunities; and speedy registration procedures. The younger students tended to emphasize those items that dealt with extracurricular activities and personal-social development concerns. Both groups expressed a high need for study skill improvement; for relaxed, informal, encouraging instructors; and for many courses providing specific job skills.

The adult student and faculty and staff comparison yielded sixty-seven items with statistical significance. The faculty and staff in general perceived the needs of adult students as much more important than the adults themselves did. Of the eighteen items assigned greater importance by the adult students, seven were related to instruction. Specifically, the adults displayed a preference for relaxed and informal instructors who provide alternative assignments and retests, incorporate audiovisual materials into instruction, and use student input to design and organize courses.

Taxonomy of Adult Student Needs. In another component of RASP, a Taxonomy of Adult Student Needs (Table 1) was developed based on the adult students' responses to the Survey of Student Needs. The taxonomy displays a three-level ordering of the survey items within five conceptual categories or facets. The facets are grouped according to the domains of learner and provider. This format was used in order to facilitate the implementation of the project's findings by the six colleges.

As indicated, the adult students expressed a high need for various improvement items listed in the Academic Survival Skills and Personal-Social Development facets. They generally exhibited a preference for certain instructor-related attitudes ("relaxed and informal" instructors), and operationally expedient services ("preregistration," "speedy registration procedures"). These findings are consistent with those of Warren and Roelfs (1972), who reported that adults are concerned with the time investment in college attendance and resent time-consuming, noninstructional activities such as complex registration procedures.

The adult students surveyed aspired to high academic achievement ("getting A's and B's"), and displayed a high need for encouragement from both within ("encouragement from instructors") and without ("encouragement from family") the institution. Since many adults return to formal study with "feelings of inadequacy about having been out of school so long" (Lenning and Hanson, 1977, p. 285), their need to succeed academically may well represent in part an attempt to substantiate their worth in a competitive academic arena. Likewise, their expressed desire for encouragement from others may be related to a need for reassurance that their academic goals are indeed credible and attainable.

Although the adult students were quite traditional in their instructional preferences ("course outlines," "course objectives," "use many examples"), they did indicate a need for some degree of flexibility in course organization ("more than one way to meet course requirements," "grades based on projects, papers, and class participation"). In addition, the adults placed a high importance on instructors who take into consideration an adult student's out-of-class responsibilities when scheduling assignments.

Anderson and Darkenwald (1979) have indicated that reentry adult students tend to be task-oriented academically. The general configuration of the items in the taxomony substantiated this notion, especially the first-order placement of improvement and instructional items and the third-order placement of extracurricular pursuits and interpersonal concerns.

Table 1. Taxonomy of Adult Student Needs

Domain	Facet	Need Continuum[1,2]		
		First Order[3]	Second Order	Third Order[4]
Learner	Academic Survival Skills M = 3.59 SD = .23	• 4.06, 1.11 Improving my study skills[5] • 3.85, 1.16 Improving my test-taking skills	• 3.62, 1.21 Learning to give better oral reports • 3.59, 1.24 Improving my vocabulary skills • 3.58, 1.32 Improving my reading skills • 3.55, 1.19 Improving my writing skills • 3.54, 1.27 Improving my math skills • 3.47, 1.22 Learning to prepare better term papers • 3.45, 1.24 Improving my note-taking skills • 3.23, 1.18 Learning to use the library facilities	
	Personal-Social Development M = 3.38 SD = .63	• 4.26, .99 Getting As and Bs in my courses • 4.09, 1.17 A place to study at home • 4.04, 1.07 Improving my concentration • 4.01, 1.10 Improving my memory • 3.90, 1.05 Acquiring a broad educational background • 3.89, 1.25 Encouragement from my family • 3.81, 1.24 Learning to organize my time better • 3.79, 1.13 Learning to set better goals for myself • 3.79, 1.14 Setting aside time every day to study	• 3.59, 1.24 Improving my motivation for my courses • 3.53, 1.26 Improving my self-confidence • 3.17, 1.31 Learning to cope with failure	• 3.07, 1.19 Working with other students on class projects • 3.03, 1.32 Keeping up with other students • 2.96, 1.30 Fitting in with other students • 2.80, 1.17 Improving my social interactions with other students • 2.66, 1.25 Studying with other students • 2.65, 1.37 Reducing my uneasiness about going to college • 2.31, 1.13 Getting together with other students after class • 2.19, 1.20 Students my own age in my classes

Provider			
Instructional Patterns M = 3.55 SD = .52	• 4.34, .92 Instructors who are personally interested in my progress • 4.04, .96 Instructors who are relaxed and informal in the classroom • 4.01, .98 Instructors who use many examples in their teaching • 4.00, 1.14 Instructors who have a realistic view of my responsibilities outside class • 3.96, .97 Encouragement from my instructors • 3.92, 1.03 Instructors who provide more than one way to meet course requirements • 3.86, 1.09 Grades based on projects, papers, and class participation instead of on tests alone	• 3.69, 1.10 Instructors who modify the course outline to satisfy student interests • 3.66, 1.02 Course objectives to guide my study • 3.66, 1.08 The use of films, tapes, and other audio-visual materials in a course • 3.49, 1.26 Being able to take re-tests to improve my grade • 3.28, 1.09 Courses with many class discussions	• 3.10, 1.17 Courses using many source materials instead of single textbooks • 3.01, 1.24 Knowing how I'm doing in relation to others in class • 2.93, 1.22 Instructors who follow the course outline very closely • 2.82, 1.05 Courses in which the instructor lectures most of the time • 2.51, 1.12 Instructors who let students decide what should be covered in a course
Administrative Policies M = 3.45 SD = .64	• 4.59, .72 Courses providing specific skills that will be useful on a job • 4.41, 1.02 Evening classes • 4.07, 1.11 Being able to obtain credit for out-of-college experiences	• 3.47, 1.36 Summer classes • 3.43, 1.24 Flexible requirements for class attendance • 3.36, 1.28 Three hour classes that meet once each week • 3.36, 1.28 Being able to take a variety of courses before deciding on a major field • 3.33, 1.26 Being able to take a course as an independent study • 3.30, 1.41 Being able to drop a course at any time without receiving a penalty grade	• 2.80, 1.29 Off-campus courses • 2.69, 1.39 Weekend classes • 2.55, 1.39 Being able to take a course with *Pass-Fail* grading instead of *A* to *F* grading

Table 1. Taxonomy of Adult Student Needs (continued)

Facet	Need Continuum[1,2] First Order[3]	Second Order	Third Order[4]
Provider			
Student Support Services M = 3.14 SD = .69	• 4.40, .86 Speedy registration procedures • 3.96, 1.12 Preregistration • 3.89, 1.22 Evening and weekend registration • 3.71, 1.15 Being able to get academic counseling	• 3.68, 1.40 Job placement services • 3.64, 1.28 Being able to get occupational counseling • 3.57, 1.45 Financial aid	• 2.99, 1.46 A place to study on campus • 2.91, 1.37 Tutoring services • 2.79, 1.37 A campus snack bar open during all class hours • 2.77, 1.34 Being able to get counseling for personal problems • 2.62, 1.26 Campus activities for students with interests similar to mine • 2.53, 1.35 A campus tour during my first semester • 2.50, 1.24 Extracurricular activites • 2.31, 1.47 Child care facilities on campus • 2.01, 1.31 Bus service to the campus

[1]Item responses scaled from *Of No Importance* (1 point) to *Of Very High Importance* (5 points).
[2]Values: Overall Mean (**OM**) = 3.41; Overall Standard Deviation (**OSD**) = .58.
[3]First Order (item mean > **OM**-.5OSD).
[4]Third Order (item mean < **OM**-.5OSD).
[5]Mean, standard deviation, and item.
Source: Joseph A. Mangano and Thomas J. Corrado, Two-Year College Development Center, State University of New York-Albany.

Although these results are generalizable across diverse educational set-tings at the two-year college level, the characteristics of the adult student sample should be kept in mind in any interpretation of the findings. The adults in the sample were students in various occupational education credit programs. The item with the highest mean (M = 4.59)—"courses providing specific skills that will be useful on the job"—reflected this orientation. Furthermore, the adults in the sample were currently enrolled students who had adjusted their life-styles to accommodate college attendance. Since they had already conformed to the conventional college fare, such items as childcare facilities, weekend classes, and off-campus courses were of low importance to them.

Adult Student Satisfaction. A final component of RASP involved an assessment of adult student satisfaction. To determine relative satisfaction, the item ratings of the Student Satisfaction Scale were ranked (high, medium, low).

Adult students in general expressed high satisfaction with mail-in regis-tration, bookstore and library services, attendance policies, course objectives and content, textbook readability, college catalogues, and overall college qual-ity. Items receiving low satisfaction ratings included ease of registration; the hours of the financial aid office; the variety of course offerings; and cafeteria, placement, tutoring, orientation, and childcare services.

Correlational and regression analyses revealed that expedient registra-tion procedures, instructor quality, course variety, and scheduling conveni-ence were most influential in determining the overall satisfactin of adult stu-dents.

Counseling Implications: Advisement and Advocacy

RASP at each of the pilot colleges was spearheaded by the steering committee assisted by the local counseling staff. This on-campus approach involved not only direct advisory efforts to assist adult students' adaptation to college but also indirect advocacy efforts to sensitize administrators and fac-ulty to the idiosyncrasies of their nontraditional clientele.

These efforts imply an expansion of the traditional counseling roles. As advisers to adult students, counselors should offer their services at convenient times and places, and should work toward easing the reentry process of adult students by providing support for and information on academic options, career changes, and lifespan development; by designating campus activities for adults and their families; and by establishing adult student networks and peer counseling services. As advocates for adult students, counselors should strive to dispel the image of the college as servant of the needs of adolescents and replace it with an image that acknowledges the importance of lifelong learning. This could be achieved through the coordination of activities to sen-sitize campus groups (administrators, faculty members, traditional college-age students) to the characteristics of older students, especially their need for scheduling convenience, expedient services, and educational and instructional alternatives.

At each of the six pilot colleges, this advisement-advocacy thrust engendered a commitment to lifelong learning, garnered campus-wide support, and proved effective in directing workable strategies to address the needs of older students. The following strategies cited by the colleges were evidenced in the general areas of administrative policies and practices, staff development, and student support services.

Administrative Policies and Practices

- Prepared campus brochures and videotape orientation materials aimed at the adult student population.
- Modified scheduling formats to accommodate adult student needs
- Increased the number of evening and summer credit and noncredit course offerings
- Developed off-campus credit and noncredit course offerings
- Initiated televised course offerings
- Improved the method of granting life-experience credit

Staff Development

- Conducted faculty and staff workshops on topics related to reentry adults
- Conducted staff development activities for adjunct faculty

Student Support Services

- Initiated speedier registration procedures
- Added a general "information booth" to the registration site
- Expanded remedial and tutorial services, financial aid counseling, job placement, career counseling, orientation services, and campus tours to accommodate part-time and evening students
- Designated a coordinator of adult student counseling and entry-level advisement services
- Initiated peer counseling services
- Organized campus activities for families of reentry adult students
- Instituted childcare services on campus
- Initiated off-campus registration, counseling, and advisement services
- Initiated a telephone counseling service providing audio tapes on such topics as test anxiety, study skill strategies, mid-life changes, stress reduction, time management, and academic reentry

Reentry adult students' preferences for flexibility, convenience, and individualization require institutional responses that are diverse, holistic, and matched to the changing needs of lifelong learners. Without the commitment of informed administrators and concerned faculty, efforts by colleges to ease the academic reentry of adult students will result in changes that at best are cosmetic and sporadic in impact.

References

Anderson, R. E., and Darkenwald, G. G. "The Adult Part-Time Learner in Colleges and Universities: A Clientele Analysis." *Research in Higher Education,* 1979, *10* (4), 357–370.

Lenning, O. T., and Hanson, G. R. "Adult Students at Two-Year Colleges: A Longitudinal Study." *Community/Junior College Research Quarterly*, 1977, *1*, 271–294.

McDermott, J. M. "Servicing the Needs of a Non-Traditional Clientele: The New Resources Approach." *Liberal Education*, 1975, *61* (2), 268–274.

Mangano, J. A., and Corrado, T. J. *Reentry Adult Student Project.* Albany, N.Y.: Two-Year College Development Center, State University of New York at Albany, 1979.

Warren, J. R., and Roelfs, P. J. *Student Reactions to College.* Palo Alto, Calif.: The College Board, 1972.

Joseph A. Mangano is project director of the Reentry Adult Student Project at the Two-Year College Development Center, State University of New York at Albany. He is former chief of the Bureau of General Continuing Education, New York State Education Department.

Thomas J. Corrado is assistant project director of the Reentry Adult Student Project and a doctoral degree candidate in educational psychology and statistics at the State University of New York at Albany.

How can a university provide counseling services to meet the needs of adult learners?

Providing Services for the Adult Learner in the University

Jane Nowak
Arthur Shriberg

"This university exists to help young people grow and develop." "This college is committed to providing our young citizens with a liberal education." These two statements taken from college catalogues convey a typical message: that colleges exist for "young people." At both of those institutions, however, the average student is in the mid-thirties.

Colleges are attracting more and more adults. In some cases, the impetus comes from an institution's need for economic survival and in others from a belief that a collegiate experience is valuable to adults as well as youth. How, then, do we adapt the mission of a college to adult learners? How do adults view the limits and expectations of their roles as students? Without careful clarification, educators and adults may mistakenly view college attendance by nontraditional students in a very narrow light, which can severely limit the quality of their educational opportunities. Educators should reexamine their purpose within a context that includes an understanding of adults as continuously developing individuals.

According to Bolles (1979), in 83 percent of the cases the trigger that causes adults to seek learning experiences is best described as a transition or

New Directions for Continuing Education, 10, 1981

change in their lives and in the remainder as a curiosity and desire to learn. Adult learners cite their most fundamental problem as lack of information about career and educational opportunities and about themselves. An individual's lack of understanding about adult life/work cycles produces "a consequent warp in the fundamental way in which he or she perceives transitions and the learning needed therein" (p. 41).

Without such understanding, an adult deciding to return to school typically struggles with personal and/or societal images of traditional students and questions the seriousness of the venture. Some see returning to school as an admission of educational or occupational deficiencies that they must atone for, and others see it at best as a means to better career marketability. Very few adults assume that returning to school can have relevance for them in terms of their personal and social growth. With this sort of mind set, they will miss many of the opportunities a college experience offers for broader development. If university staff members believe in creating an environment as rich as possible in a variety of ways for all students, they should make this explicit and available for all learners.

Student development workers are in an ideal position to coordinate the communication among all groups involved—faculty, administrators, students, and themselves—to meaningfully address the needs of adult learners within the college setting. Student development workers are the student affairs division staff, and have direct contact with students. It is important that student development professionals begin to view the institution itself as their client (Conyne and others, 1979), as well as continuing their work with individual students. The same principles that are applied to individuals can be utilized to facilitate institutional change for the benefit of those individuals. To do this, it is helpful for adult educators to assist student development workers in reassessing their own mission in the context of an understanding of adult learners and to touch base with the foundations of the helping professions that have enabled them to be of help to all ages and classes of people.

Counseling Principles and the Adult Learner

It is imperative that educational administrators understand the nature of what counseling professionals do. It is equally necessary that counselors become attuned to the variety of needs of administrators regarding their students. Without mutual understanding and cooperative flexibility, successful collaboration to provide student services will be lacking.

The term "counselor" is applied to various individuals in a college setting. Admissions counselors, financial aid counselors, career planning counselors, and psychological counselors are all involved to varying degrees in what is called a counseling process. Each of these individuals is essentially a student development professional. Since terminology and the intent of any given job title varies across institutions, let us look more specifically at the ingredients of helping relationships in order to identify roles and clarify the nature of the counseling process.

Essentially, counseling is "intended to explore the [client's] feelings, increase his self-understanding, and eventually help him discover new and more effective ways of living" (Shaffer and Shoben, 1967). Its purpose is to facilitate choices that will enhance a person's later development (Tyler, 1969). In most schools of thought, it is generally acknowledged that people will grow or change if there is a suitable psychological environment in which to do so. Lewis (1978), Rogers (1961), and others have cited qualities and behaviors that help create such an atmosphere: genuineness on the part of the helper, nonjudgmental acceptance of each part of the client's experience, and understanding of the nature of the client's perceptions.

Student development workers help facilitate students' choices in ways ranging from information giving to career planning to discussing personal crises. Varying degrees of skill and professional preparation are required at different levels. An institutional environment needs to include all of these components in a well-integrated network. If a college is to help students explore and understand themselves, all faculty and counselors involved must understand the nature of the student's perceptions and needs and accept them unconditionally. They must be generally interested and committed to their students' welfare and growth.

Just as a psychological counselor strives to meet and work with individuals from their specific starting points, a college must make itself aware of and be able to meet its adult clientele in their current situations. A continuing education administrator cannot assume that voluminous information giving is sufficient to launch adult students into a well-rounded college experience. Satisfactory services can be achieved by student development professionals, administrators, and faculty members working together to develop a range of services that can have dimensions appropriate for the entire continuum of adult developmental needs.

Psychological Needs of Adult Learners

Something of a paradox often exists between what adults feel and what they think they should feel upon embarking on a college experience. They may think that since they are mature they should know what to do and have few of the questions or hesitancies to which they feel a youthful college student would be entitled. Sometimes the fear of admitting to uncertainties deters them from becoming involved at all. If they are able to get past this, however, many adults find themselves flooded with the same attitudes and feelings about school that they had in their youth. In the case of an individual for whom school was a creative and enjoyable experience, this may not present much of a problem. But when the individual has experienced school as threatening, oppressive, and anxiety-producing, it is likely that these same feelings will shape expectations of a return to college.

Many adults went to school in the days when students were expected to be passive absorbers who deferred to the judgments of all-knowing educators. The educators told them what to do and how to do it; creativity and original thinking were rarely sanctioned. A student would never assume the right to question a teacher about purposes or methods. A college environment of today is typically very different, but if returning adult students are not aided in developing a new concept of a student's role in college, they may never feel free to participate in a more active, questioning way. Faculty members involved in teaching new adult learners can have an invaluable impact by reaching out to them to discuss new and old learning philosophies and by encouraging them to try on the new role. If this is done with sensitivity and respect, adult students are likely to thrive. If the adults feel condescended to or ridiculed, the results could be devastating. If not addressed at all, the gap in expectations could result in increased anxiety for adults who realize that the way of playing the game has changed but cannot quite make the moves necessary for the transition.

The teachers and administrators with whom adult students have daily contact are often the first persons to whom the students will express their concerns. By taking the student and his or her questions seriously, the educator encourages the student to pursue those questions or concerns. Receptive attitudes and willingness to listen to the student add to the student's confidence in continuing to explore resources. If faculty members or administrators take an attitude of "I don't know the answer so I can't get involved in the question," they may be setting an example for students who are also afraid of the many unknowns with which they are confronted. Students who feel that no one wants to be "bothered" with their questions often do not bother to pursue the questions themselves.

Orientation and the Adult Learner

Most often, the primary services necessary simply to register for a course (admission, advisement, registration, and financing) are compartmentalized and handled by separate offices. The numerous questions adults have about returning to school, however, are by no means compartmentalized. Adults wishing to sign up for the first time are typically not at all versed in the bureaucracy with which they must deal in order to accomplish this one task. Questions are often tied up with fears and apprehensions that become compounded when they realize that not only do they not know the answers to their questions, but they also have no idea whom to ask. Any arrangement of student services capable of preventing this situation is desirable. It is very helpful to have specific individuals on campus designated as contact persons who can take the time to explain all that is involved. They can also help to identify some of the concerns of the student and either provide direct attention to those concerns or facilitate smooth referrals to the appropriate office. Preentry orientation workshops can introduce potential adult students to the specific people involved at each step of the entry, advisement, and registration process, and provide step-by-step written guidelines on what must be done, by whom, and in what location in order to sign up for courses.

In order to help new adult learners feel more comfortable and lessen apprehensiveness, an orientation program utilizing peers trained in basic helping skills might be useful. To overcome feeling different from and not accepted by typical college students, returning adults might be paired with traditional students in a task-oriented or group setting that would allow interaction and feedback in a structured way. A supper with spouses, campus tours, and mini-dramas on coping with various concerns could be a part of a returnee orientation (Scott and Holt, 1976).

Many returning adults make the assumption that they will proceed with their college efforts at the same degree of proficiency they had when they were last in school. Even though years of life and professional experience may have altered or refined their reading, writing, mathematical, or analytical skills, a memory such as having flunked their eighth grade English class can be a source of shameful apprehension. Adult learners can benefit from an early opportunity to test out how their skills have fared and to build confidence in their ability to transfer much of their life experience into functional classroom tools.

In addition, in coordinating appropriate services for adult students, care should be taken to provide brush-up opportunities in areas such as library use and term paper writing. Recent high school graduates may have many of these skills at their fingertips, but someone out of school for a while is more likely to have had little or no necessity to remember such details. Tutorial assistance should be offered by student development workers who are aware of the different techniques by which adult learners learn and who can deal with the emotional issues that may be blocking academic progress. If we want to help students progress in their development, we must meet them at the point at which they stand.

Developmental Tasks of Adult Learners

It is unrealistic and undesirable for teachers, administrators, or staff to attempt to do psychological counseling without the appropriate professional preparation. But is is also wasteful not to take advantage of and enhance the interactions and relationships of college life that already exist. Student development professionals can work with faculty members in seminars designed to help them refine basic listening and clarification skills, identify appropriate campus referral sources, and examine the stereotypes with which they may be dealing with adult students. Student development workers can work with adult students individually or in groups to help them understand their feelings about their student role. They can also help adults understand their situation through course work that surveys sociological and psychological perspectives on adults returning to school. Assertiveness training programs can give adults practice in expressing their feelings in an active, appropriate manner.

The expectations with which most adults grew up seldom included the idea of returning to school in their middle years. For many years, even career development theory and research were confined to the developmental tasks of youth. Adults were either indirectly omitted or directly portrayed as spending their time in maintaining whatever career they set out to pursue in their youth. The idea of choosing to change direction was hardly mentioned, and retraining in mid-life was usually seen as the result of changes in demand, such as replacement by automation.

In seeking to attract adult students, educators need to expand their assumptions about why adults return to school. In dealing with returning adult learners, it is advantageous to build in interactions and extended contact with professionals who can identify adults who are questioning themselves because their lives are turning out differently from what they had expected. Those who find themselves starting a new direction need not have a negative self-concept. Speakers in a seminar series, for example, could address recent research and theoretical knowledge on adult development cycles and transitions developed by people such as Knox (1977), Nayman (1980), and Gould (1978). Following the presentations, student development workers could lead discussions to examine personal feelings and perceptions regarding this information.

In addition to new life stages, specific life crises can prompt a decision to return to school or affect adult students when they are in school. Of the 83 percent of the cases of reentry because of transitions or life changes, 56 percent are related to work, 34 percent to changes in family life, and 6 percent to changes in personal health or that of a partner (Bolles, 1979). Divorce, business setbacks, children leaving home, and retirement are examples of events that can affect an adult learner's ability to function in school. Professional individual or group counseling as well as informal support groups are important services that colleges can provide to adult learners. Social events of either a general nature or focused around a specific interest area can give adults a chance to form relationships with peers otherwise difficult to meet on campus.

Toward a Smoother Network

The range of possibilities by which the principles and methods of counseling can be extended into all student service areas is limited only by one's creative imagination. Crucial to the task of making these possibilities a reality is cooperation among administrators valuing different areas of expertise, a student development staff well versed in the needs of adult learners and willing to train others in appropriate helper skill areas, and a coordinating person or system that is receptive to the needs and suggestions of adult students, educational administrators, and counselors. Student development workers must understand and accept the needs of continuing education administrators concerning recruitment, retention, and program development for adult students and must be genuinely interested in and committed to addressing those needs. Continuing education administrators need to understand the nature of the work done by student development personnel and provide them with information and resources that can help them discover more effective ways of dealing with adult students. Together, student development personnel and continuing education administrators can shape the institutional environment to be more supportive of adult learners. It is vital to represent the nature and needs of adult students in college-wide policy decisions and to consistently educate and integrate faculty into adult learner programs and concerns.

The extent to which counselors, administrators, and faculty members can work together to meet the needs of adult learners will influence the quality of the educational experience that the university can offer them.

References

Bolles, R. "Training for Transition: Changing Careers." *Change,* 1979, *11* (5), 40–44.
Conyne, R., and others. "The Campus Environment as Client: A New Direction for College Counselors." *Journal of College Student Personnel,* 1979, *20* (5), 437–442.
Gould, R. *Transformations: Growth and Change in Adult Life.* New York: Simon & Schuster, 1978.
Knox, A. B. *Adult Development and Learning: A Handbook on Individual Growth and Competence in the Adult Years for Education and the Helping Professions.* San Francisco: Jossey-Bass, 1977.
Lewis, J. *To Be a Therapist: The Teaching and Learning.* New York: Brunner/Mazel, 1978.
Nayman, R. "Student Development Services and the Adult Learner." In A. Shriberg (Ed.), *New Directions for Student Services: Providing Student Services for the Adult Learner,* no. 11. San Francisco: Jossey-Bass, 1980.
Rogers, C. *On Becoming a Person.* Boston: Houghton Mifflin, 1961.
Scott, R., and Holt, L. "The New Wave: A College Responds to Women Returnees." *Phi Delta Kappan,* 1976, *58* (4), 338–339.
Shaffer, L., and Shoben, E. "Common Aspects of Psychotherapy." In B. Berenson and R. Carkhuff (Eds.), *Sources of Gain in Counseling and Psychotherapy.* New York: Holt, Rinehart and Winston, 1967.
Tyler, L. *The Work of the Counselor.* New York: Appleton Century Crofts, 1969.

Jane Nowak, a counselor at Seton Hall University, administers a career counseling project for the adult learner population. She is a doctoral degree student in psychology at Columbia University.

Arthur Shriberg is vice-president for student affairs at Seton Hall University. He is the editor of a Jossey-Bass sourcebook entitled New Directions for Student Services: Providing Student Services for the Adult Learner *(no. 11, 1980) and a consultant in this field.*

With university commitment, comprehensive counseling
services can provide the key to attracting and
retaining adult learners.

Comprehensive
Counseling Services

Nancy C. Gelling

Recent writings on counseling adult learners make a strong case for the importance of continuing education counseling and information services. Most university continuing education divisions, however, devote only a token effort to
counseling services (Grabowski, 1976; Knox and Farmer, 1977).

This chapter provides a case example of Syracuse University's strong
commitment to the counseling role of its continuing education division, called
University College. It indicates the range of counseling services that have
evolved for adult learners.

The current variety of services is in contrast with the early days of
counseling following World War I, when university efforts consisted mainly of
course instructors or the dean of the graduate school approving enrollment in
credit courses to make sure that part-time students were in the right courses.
However, by the end of World War II, institutional commitment to continuing education was sufficiently strong that University College appointed a
counselor of students who had had preparation in counseling and student personnel services (Tolley, 1977). Since then, comprehensive counseling and student services have been developed that involve many academic and support
units throughout the university and help attract and retain adult students.

Today the counseling center is a port of entry for adults from the community who want to explore educational opportunities through University
College and a point of continuing contact for adult students until they achieve

New Directions for Continuing Education, 10, 1981

their educational objectives. Staff consists of the director, five full-time and two part-time professional counselors, and seven peer counselors.

The core of the center's activities are the individual counseling sessions, as reflected in more than five thousand appointments with the professional counselors last year. In addition, information is provided over the telephone, especially by peer counselors (Arbeiter and others, 1978).

The assistance that is provided varies greatly. For adults who are unfamiliar with the university, information is given about courses, programs, procedures, and degree requirements. During the registration periods three times each year, counselors and some of the faculty members who teach through University College assist adults with the registration process. For adults who want to matriculate in a degree program, the center serves as an admissions office and recommends applicants to the university admissions office.

New students do not have to become degree candidates immediately; counselors help them select courses and credit or noncredit options as they explore possible majors and generally gain confidence. Because course requirements can be met in various ways (class, television, independent study, radio, newspaper, audiotapes, credit by examination), counselors help adults consider and select alternatives. In addition, counselors maintain personnel files for all University College students, act on student petitions for exceptions to rules and regulations, provide a student handbook to orient new students, assist students who must withdraw or who experience academic difficulties, conduct free study skills workshops, certify that applicants for graduation have met degree requirements, and arrange for an annual commencement dinner to honor graduates.

The extensive contact counselors have with adult students enables them to personalize the relationship between the student and the college. To do so effectively requires that counselors be in touch with both the students and the institution. With their other commitments and no-nonsense approach to education, adults appreciate the efforts of counselors to interpret institutional expectations and standards, to minimize unnecessary red tape, and to provide encouragement and support. Peer counselors are helpful in responding to telephone inquiries with accurate information, which they as experienced adult students are especially able to give, along with personal support (Gelling, 1979).

The ability of counselors to be responsive and flexible in assisting adult students depends on maintaining effective relationships with many campus offices—such as admissions, student affairs, alumni, and academic deans—that have delegated authority to the counseling center to act on their behalf. For instance, the director of the counseling center is also an associate director of admissions and is able to decide on admissions of adult part-time students.

Center staff also work with University College student groups, such as an advisory council, an honor society, the peer counselors, and an alumni group. These groups sponsor activities such as a speakers bureau to interpret the college to the community, events to recognize outstanding University College students and alumni, and fund raising to provide financial assistance for adult part-time students. In addition, counselors are able to distill information about educational needs of the clientele and to transmit it to University College program administrators to use in modifying the offerings.

The central position that counselors enjoy results from their avoiding the temptation to remain aloof from the programming of University College and instead embracing the opportunity to be involved in the total marketing effort. The relationships with individual students are of course client-centered and confidential, but center staff engage in many additional activities that contribute to the visibility and service of the counseling center and thus of the college.

Visibility for the counseling function is achieved in various ways. Most of the television, radio, and newspaper advertising for University College features counselors and students. The basic theme is consistent: Adult students will receive individual attention, and counselors who know the system and care about adult students provide information, encouragement, support, and assistance at the very first inquiry and throughout students' association with University College. Counselors also have personal contact with potential participants by serving on community committees, speaking to local groups, attending transfer days at community colleges, and visiting local industries to counsel their employees.

The core of University College is helping adults learn. The total marketing effort of the college is designed to attract and retain adults who want to continue their education. The counseling center epitomizes and personalizes this service orientation. A recent marketing survey confirmed the centrality of the counseling function in the marketing and programming efforts of the college. Center staff members provide the leadership for college-wide attention to counseling to which program administrators, faculty members, students, and people from elsewhere in the university and the community contribute.

References

Arbeiter, S., and others. *Telephone Counseling for Home-Based Adults.* New York: The College Board, 1978.
Gelling, N. C. "Peer Counseling Program." *Innovations in Continuing Education: Award-Winning New Programs.* Washington, D.C.: National University Extension Association and the American College Testing Program, 1979.
Grabowski, S. M. "Educational Counseling of Adults." *Adult Leadership,* 1976, *24* (7), 225-227, 249.
Knox, A. B., and Farmer, H. S. "Overview of Counseling and Information Services for Adult Learners." *International Review of Education,* 1977, *23* (4), 387-414.
Tolley, W. P. *The Adventure of Learning.* Syracuse, N.Y.: Syracuse University Press, 1977.

Nancy C. Gelling is director of counseling and student services, University College, Syracuse University.

A large hospital can tap many sources to help hospital staff with educational, career, and job-related concerns.

Who Does Career Counseling in a Large Hospital?

Alan G. Cotzin
Betty R. Radcliffe

A hospital provides a unique and challenging environment in which to conduct educational and career counseling for the staff. A large hospital is comparable in many ways to a small town. It requires the services of almost every type of person — professional, skilled, and unskilled — so that it may function effectively in providing top-quality patient care. In many instances, it also provides an educational and research function. The staff includes nursing personnel, allied health professionals, service and maintenance personnel, skilled tradespeople, managers, and administrators. These groups require a diversified approach to educational and career counseling services.

The University of Michigan Hospital meets this challenge by taking a multifaceted approach to provide counseling services for staff. Some services are provided indirectly to employees, but the majority are provided directly through the Office of Human Resources Development (HRD), which is a part of the Medical Campus Personnel Office. Counseling is also available from the employee's immediate supervisor and from a number of other sources.

Office of Human Resources Development

The Office of Human Resources Development (HRD) was established in January 1978 as a result of a firm commitment from the hospital director

New Directions for Continuing Education, 10, 1981

and personnel administrator. One of the first new staff members recruited was a specialist in the career development area.

Approximately 70 percent of a hospital's budget is devoted to human resources. Because health care professionals are asking for more job fulfillment and satisfaction, the hospital director and personnel administrator believed that career development was an extremely high priority in the development of a comprehensive office of HRD. Administrators in large institutions are becoming more aware of the need to provide career planning opportunities for their employees (Walker, 1980).

The career development coordinator provides the focal point for hospital personnel who desire assistance in career planning beyond help that is given by the immediate supervisor. All services are provided on a confidential basis and without charge to the employee.

Workshops. In order to maximize the effort of the career development coordinator, HRD instituted a series of workshops to guide employees through the career awareness and development process. The Career Awareness Workshop consists of three two-hour sessions that help employees to focus on their skills and abilities, set realistic career goals for themselves, and develop realistic and practical action plans.

These sessions are conducted for employees in each general job family with the hope that a support group of persons with similar interests and concerns can be generated. One of the main values of this type of workshop is the sharing and interaction among the participants. Techniques such as the wire life-line (writing a description of past life events), the writing of the person's retirement speech, and an action plan are used in the program. Six-month group follow-up sessions have also been held to review and revise action plans. Career development specialists are now emphasizing the need to review and update goals and action plans (Kaye, 1980).

Employees who attend any of the workshops must spend their own time. A balance of the institution's participation and the employee's commitment to career development is essential in order for the process to work. Other workshops that are offered, usually during the lunch hour, include résumé writing, job interviewing, and job-finding techniques. Through such workshops, HRD has been able to reduce the amount of time the career development coordinator spends in individual counseling.

Vocational Testing. We feel that it is most important that the employees be given standardized feedback concerning their career interests. Through a cooperative arrangement with the Department of Guidance and Counseling in the School of Education, we offer free vocational testing to any hospital employee. This program consists of an initial interview followed by a standardized test (usually the Strong-Campbell). Later, a feedback session is arranged. The counselors in the Department of Guidance and Counseling are master's degree students who are working under the supervision of the university's faculty. The service has proved beneficial both to the hospital and to the school of education: The hospital is able to offer free vocational testing and the School of

Education receives subjects for training their students. The subjects have had experience in the work force and usually have obligations and perspectives other than a college undergraduate who is trying to decide on a vocation.

Educational Opportunity Fair. Many hospital staff members have little or no knowledge of the various educational institutions in our area where they could pursue further formal education. The university does offer a tuition reimbursement program and three hours per week of paid release time for people to acquire additional college course work that is job-related or within a field to which the employee can reasonably aspire.

In an effort to inform staff of the many educational institutions they might attend, University Hospital presents an annual educational opportunity fair. All schools and colleges and educational support groups in the area are invited for a one-day exhibit in the hospital cafeteria. Last year, twenty-two organizations participated in the fair, with one school handing out 500 schedules and catalogues. Employees have found this an extremely helpful method of gaining information about schools and having questions answered by representatives of those educational institutions. In addition, the educational institutions have found the experience an extremely positive way of marketing their programs. The hospital also publishes a booklet that describes the participating institutions and summarizes the programs, costs, and registration dates. Extra copies of this booklet are used as a handout for employees who participate in our other career development programs and activities.

Career Resource Library. HRD has started to develop a career resource library to provide a centralized point for hospital staff to obtain career development information. Included in the library are catalogues of area colleges and universities, copies of test-preparation books, books on job-finding techniques, résumé writing, and other related documents. HRD also subscribes to the Michigan Occupational Information System (MOIS), which provides the employee with another source of information about career interests and information related to job possibilities. The components of the MOIS occupational searching system include a questionnaire on job interests, a personal profile, a workbook, and a microfiche file that describes 350 occupations covering 1,400 specific job titles. The workbook is used to match the staff member's personal profile with titles of occupations. The microfiche provides detailed information about the job, employment potential, number of people needed in the field, description of the job, working environment, positive and negative aspects of the work, education required, and schools where one can obtain this education.

The information is updated annually and has been found useful by the employees and the career development coordinator. The employment section of the Medical Campus Personnel Office also assists in this effort at the request of the Michigan Department of Education by reviewing information on MOIS for accuracy and currency. Thus, the hospital is not only a user of the MOIS service but also provides basic information to the Michigan system. The Office of Human Resources Development has used the MOIS program as a job search feature in career fairs.

58

Individual Counseling. HRD provides confidential individual career counseling for any hospital staff member. This activity represents 20 to 25 percent of the time commitment of the career development coordinator. Although this is a key service to individuals, many of the described activities of the career development coordinator are a supplement or substitute for individual counseling. Counseling is provided during all shifts by appointment. The follow-up activities, such as participation in a résumé-writing course, a career awareness workshop, or an educational opportunity fair, as well as vocational testing, may be outcomes of the counseling. The career development coordinator also provides an important link to the employment section by apprising the counselee of job openings and by informing the employment representative of the interests of hospital staff people in moving to the positions. The initiation of other activities and programs such as career path and human resource planning should further reduce the amount of time spent in individual counseling.

Tuition Reimbursement. A program to monitor tuition reimbursement allocations is in the planning stages at University Hospital. For many years, a large amount of hospital money has been spent on the tuition reimbursement program, without, however, linking the employees' educational program to the promotional system. The hospital is now initiating activities to help the employee change positions based on continuing education and is offering counseling services to people entering the tuition reimbursement program. HRD also plans to provide information to hospital staff members on the viability of the program, other places where a similar degree may be obtained, and the need for the types of proficiencies that the person wishes to acquire.

Other Services. The career development coordinator also supervises the general educational development program that is given in conjunction with the local school system. Hospital employees are allowed paid release time each week to work toward the attainment of a high school diploma. HRD also participates in the university's annual women's career fair and has assisted in career awareness activities for minorities. In the future, HRD is looking toward the area of career path and human resource planning to provide a wide range of career development opportunities for all hospital staff members.

Performance Planning and Evaluation

The hospital has recently implemented a mandatory performance planning and evaluation program. This process is based upon an agreed-upon performance plan, usually negotiated annually between the employee and the supervisor at the beginning of a review. The performance plan includes major areas of responsibilities, objectives, measurement criteria, and priorities.

Another component of this program is the employee development form, which focuses on either the employee's career interests or on improving the employee's job performance. The hospital's approach to performance planning includes evaluating all managers and supervisors on their activities concerning employee development. The managers and supervisors become counselors in the areas of career planning, career development, and on-the-job performance improvement. Not only must the supervisors complete the forms, they must also provide documentation to their managers on actions taken to help their employees grow and develop professionally. The Office of Human Resources Development, which is coordinating the training for this new system, has developed a resource guide to assist managers and supervisors in implementing the program. Part of the performance planning and evaluation program is ongoing coaching and counseling of employees by their managers and supervisors. Burack and Mathys (1980) recently pinpointed the high degree of skill needed by a manager in coaching and counseling employees in order to increase their commitment to achieving personal and institutional goals.

The performance planning and evaluation program is a major effort in institutionalizing educational counseling and career development for employees in the hospital. HRD expects that the career development coordinator will train managers and supervisors in methods of providing career counseling to their employees.

Management Development Assessment Center. University Hospital is the first in the country to implement a hospital-specific management development assessment center. The assessment center uses simulations of management activities to develop specific feedback to the employees on their management strengths and weaknesses. The program, which has been instituted for the first-line supervisors, can be used for selection or employee development. Six candidates participate in a center; they are observed by three trained assessors who are usually managers at the department level or above.

We provide staff members with specific feedback in nine skill areas: leadership, decision making, decisiveness, adaptability, organizing and planning, sensitivity, perception, oral communication, and written communication. The employee receives oral and written feedback on individual performance and then is given a specific career development plan based upon the findings of the assessment center. This information is confidential and is shared with the employee's supervisor only with the employee's permission. Some employees choose to have the feedback session conducted with their supervisor present while others prefer a private consultation.

Education and Training Programs. Because HRD offers a variety of education and training programs in the hospital, employees see other staff members in the Office of Human Resources Development as resources for counseling. People who attend the sixty-one hour management development core program, which is mandatory for all new hospital managers and supervisors, find that the HRD staff provides them with a valuable resource. They can seek counseling with a staff member and discuss their problems and concerns in a nonthreatening, nonsupervisory relationship. Clerks and secretaries have found the instructors in the clerical program helpful in providing counseling.

HRD offers an employee relations training program two and a half days long, taught with the assistance of personnel representatives from the staff relations and union relations sections of the Medical Campus Personnel Office. Almost the entire staff of these two offices assists us in presenting the program so that personnel representatives will have an opportunity to meet with hospital managers and supervisors in a setting which is nonthreatening and not related to problems. This contributes to a more effective communication system between the personnel representatives and the line management personnel. In addition, HRD personnel representatives provide counseling to any hospital staff member for a job-related or non–job-related problem.

Faculty and Staff Assistance Program. Through the University of Michigan Staff Benefits Office, hospital employees may participate in the Faculty and Staff Assistance Program (FASAP). This program is designed to aid employees who are having problems outside the work setting that are affecting their on-the-job performance, such as marital, financial, and emotional problems as well as alcoholism and drug abuse. Participation in this program may also become a condition of employment, the last major opportunity for an employee to improve his or her on-the-job performance. In addition to counseling in the hospital, the staff members of FASAP provide linkage with the community resources. Supervisors may also meet with the FASAP coordinators to receive counseling and guidance concerning the best methods of approaching employees who are having these types of problems.

Organizational Development. Another means of making contact with the employees for the purpose of providing career education or other types of counseling can be through organizational development intervention activities. At any time, HRD may be called upon to provide organizational development service. Often these interventions lead to counseling of both management and staff in a wide range of areas. Thus, the organizational development specialists provide linkage between the various services described in this chapter and the staff members who are involved in the organizational development project.

Summary

Providing counseling services in a major hospital setting requires a variety of services to meet the employees' needs on an indirect and direct basis. The services must be available twenty-four hours a day, seven days a week, in order to meet the needs of all members of the work force. Through a coordinated career development program, a well-developed performance planning and evaluation program, and many other services, HRD has been able to implement a comprehensive approach to employee counseling.

References

Burack, E., and Mathys, N. *Career Management in Organizations*. Lake Forest, Ill.: Brace-Park, 1968.
Kaye, B. "How You Can Help Employees Formulate Their Career Goals." *Personnel Journal*, 1980, *59* (5), 368–373.
Walker, J. W. *Human Resource Planning*. New York: McGraw-Hill, 1980.

Alan G. Cotzin is the director of the Office of Human Resources Development at University Hospital and lecturer in the School of Public Health at the University of Michigan. His office provides programs in management development, staff training, and career counseling.

Betty R. Radcliffe is the career development coordinator at University Hospital. Her responsibilities include individual counseling, career-planning workshops, an educational fair, and career fairs.

A three-dimensional approach to counseling services
resulted in significant increases in adult learner participation
in educational opportunities.

Diversity by Demand

Ruth J. Brenner

The end of the draft in 1973 was a historic event that ushered in the all-volunteer military force. Speaking to a group of educators, Assistant Secretary of Defense Roger T. Kelly (1973) indicated that improvement of educational opportunities in the military had made this possible. In addition, he reported studies that had identified educational opportunity as one of the main motivators in influencing youth to enter the military service. Educational opportunity became and has remained a primary military recruiting tool. Today, competition among industry, higher education, and the military continues to be keen in a declining youth population. As the most publicized incentive for attracting volunteers to choose the military today, educational benefits depend on counseling services to deliver the recruiter's promise. Diversity is demanded of the educator who aspires to effectively assist the adult learner in the military achieve educational goals, according to Rose (1979).

Commitment to Opportunity

A statement of human goals issued by the Department of Defense became the basis of a personnel policy that emphasizes educational opportunity as necessary to the individual, the agency, and the nation. Kelly's phrase "to provide opportunity for everyone . . . to rise as high . . . as talent and diligence will take him" (1973, p. 3) became the cornerstone that created a commitment to extending educational opportunity in a more planned comprehensive manner.

To meet the range of educational aspirations that attract individuals to the all-volunteer force is a challenging task. Opportunity must be available to those who wish to continue formal education as well as those who need to remediate educational deficits in order to accomplish career goals. Education services have the task of providing the counseling and tailoring the programs that mesh with individual needs and organizational requirements. Specifically, the Air Force mandates that a program that ranges from high school through graduate study be accessible and feasible during the average duty assignment on each installation.

Educational opportunity is considered a part of the enlistment contract and guaranteed to be available to the individual in off-duty time. When these provisions are not honored, the individual can request that the contract be voided. Because of the nature of many military operations and mobility requirements, innovations in delivery systems must be continuously explored. To help each individual to identify and achieve educational goals in off-duty time requires a comprehensive and systematic counseling approach. Massey (1979) strongly supports viable alternatives that require ingenuity in both individual facilitation and responsive program development for a highly heterogeneous population.

About 80 percent of those who enter the military return to civilian life after enlistment. The total package of skill training and educational opportunity meets the career education goals supported by the Department of Education. As the largest single employer of youth, the armed forces is committed to the position that those who volunteer to defend the nation will return to society with enhanced skills.

Dealing with Diversity

Need, opportunity, and desire are not sufficient for adults to engage in continuing education. These were findings of Aslanian and Brickell in a major study of 1,500 adults (1980). Therefore, a significant factor in meeting the educational commitments of the military to the individual is management of counseling. Allocation of professional resources programmed for maximum impact during a period of transition can undergird the counseling function. A descriptive model of counseling proposed by Morrill, Oetting, and Hurst (1974) applies to various settings. The three dimensions proposed were the target, purpose, and method of intervention. This comprehensive model has proved very useful in developing a strategy for fully utilizing limited professional resources to facilitate the achievement of educational goals on Eglin Air Force Base. The typical allocation by counseling activity and time that have proved productive when directed at the transitional phases of changing jobs, promotions, and so forth, are shown in Table 1.

Target of Intervention. The counselor in the educational setting for the military adult learner can choose to intervene at any one of four levels identified by Morrill, Oetting, and Hurst (1974): individual, primary group,

Table 1. Management of Counseling Function by Activities and Time

	Percent	Hours in One Month
Counseling Activities	60	90–100
One-to-one counseling relationship	50–55	85–90
Related referral activities/consultations—OJT		
supervisors, ed. staff, test proctors, etc.	5–10	10–15
Guidance Activities	18	30
Group briefings	6 +	10
Visiting work areas	6 +	10
Coordinating with other staff agencies	6 +	10
Administrative Activities	10	16
Maintaining guidance counselor cumulative		
appointment/counseling session records	5	7 +
Special reports, research projects, related activity,		
telephone calls, etc.	5	8 +
Leave, Medical Appointments	7 +	12
Related Activities	5	8
Self-development, professional seminars, etc.		

associational group, and institutional. Intervention at all levels has expanded resources and enhanced opportunity for Eglin and adult learners.

Individual. The attempt to serve the individual either on a one-to-one or a small group basis is the major intervention strategy used by the military education counselor. The primary purpose is to facilitate positive changes in the individual and, when carried out in a group, the focus is still directed at individual development using group methods. All military personnel in transition to a new station are informed about educational opportunities on the new military base, and they are encouraged to further refine their individual career goals.

Primary Group. The influence family and friends have on individual behavior and the level of involvement in educational activities is directly related to perceptions within primary groups. A counseling strategy may be directed at informing or assisting family and friends as indicated. All new arrivals are encouraged to seek a support group of those presently enrolled in their units and invited to involve spouse and friends in educational plans.

Associational Group. The more organized groups are targeted for intervention at regular intervals, for example, when first-term airmen are promoted to sergeant. Groups with interests and goals in common are routinely approached to increase awareness of opportunities to satisfy needs.

Institutional. Intervention at this level is directed at key organizational elements to provide a system linkage that will result in support for individual achievement. This approach also facilitates a flow of information that enables responsive programs that accommodate mission constraints and off-duty opportunities.

Purpose of Intervention. The purpose of counseling for any given individual at various times may be remediation, prevention, or development, often with overlap in many situations.

Remediation. Counseling and testing of individuals who have difficulty progressing in training provide opportunities to build basic skills. Those with marginal achievement scores at time of enlistment are routinely tested and provided skill development as required.

Prevention. Counseling and orientation of newly enrolled students are essentially directed at prevention. Proper selection of courses to meet individual goals that allow for success is a vital factor for the reentry adult.

Development. The primary purpose of all counseling services is to promote positive growth. Clarifying purpose and identifying resources help to move adults from their present situation to a desired situation.

Method of Intervention. The method of reaching the target varies with purpose and resources available. To reach the large number of constituents in a military institution, it is essential that the method extend the range of influence of the counselor to the maximum extent possible. Although primarily involved directly with the target population, the counselor must also consult with and train others to deliver full services. In addition, the media provide a vehicle for intervention that should not be underestimated.

Direct Service. Professional involvement here is primarily used in situations where experienced judgment and counseling skills are required. Examples are initial goal setting, special program entry, or test interpretation.

Consultation and Training. A comprehensive training program for educators provides ongoing service to a large number of clients, as well as a variety of role models to reach various groups of individuals. Regular consultation with key personnel in work units also results in many supporting services being delivered by those who work with the clients on a regular basis for other purposes.

Media. Informational brochures are used widely to address specific programs. All sources of news media are used extensively. Videotapes using peer models are a popular source of information about career and educational opportunities.

Morrill, Oetting, and Hurst (1974) point out that overriding all dimensions is the requirement to regularly assess needs and evaluate effectiveness of intervention strategies, the priority of targets selected, and efficiency of method of delivery.

Conclusion

Exception is the rule in counseling service personnel who range from eighteen to fifty-eight years of age and from eighth grade to graduate level of education. Opportunity exists only if access is assured. When counselor activity is devoted to system intervention as well as facilitating individual growth, the necessary flexibility and initiative are provided. To view services on a three-dimensional basis provides a systematic method to ensure educational opportunities equal to the recruiting promise.

References

Aslanian, C. B., and Brickell, H. M. *Americans in Transition.* New York: The College Board, 1980.
Kelly, R. T. *Educational Opportunities in the All-Volunteer Force Era.* Address presented to National Association of Secondary School Principals, Dallas, February 6, 1973.
Massey, T. B. "Delivering Voluntary Off-Duty Education." *Continuum,* 1979, *44* (2), 11–13.
Morrill, W. H., Oetting, E. R., and Hurst, J. C. "Dimensions of Counselor Functioning." *Personnel and Guidance Journal,* 1974, *52* (6), 354–359.
Rose, M. R. "A Unique and Precious Partnership." *Continuum,* 1979, *44* (2), 5–6.

Ruth J. Brenner was recently medically retired as chief of the Education Services Branch, Eglin Air Force Base, Florida. Nine years of developing a comprehensive program of educational opportunity by implementing a three-dimensional approach to counseling services has resulted in adult learner participation increases from 500 to over 3,000 enrollments each term in programs ranging from high school through graduate study.

*When public school funds are limited, how do we provide
adequate counseling for adult learners?*

Counseling Services
for Adults in the
Public Schools

Frank R. DiSilvestro
Mary Grcich Williams

The title of this chapter could very easily have been "Meeting the Counseling
Needs of Adult Learners in the Public Schools During a Time of Diminishing
Resources and Programs." It is no secret that in many public school settings
the importance of providing counseling services for adult learners is considered marginal when compared to the need to generate revenues from numbers
of students enrolled. Resources for counseling services are frequently sacri-
ficed to provide instruction to as many students as possible, or the resources
are used for recruitment and marketing in order to gain additional students.
Darkenwald (1980, p. 202) described the situation as follows:

> In public school adult education settings, counseling is provided princi-
> pally for adults enrolled in basic education, high school completion,
> and vocational training programs. Thus, limited resources for counsel-
> ing, mostly from state and federal sources, are allocated almost exclu-
> sively to assist disadvantaged and/or undereducated adults . . . . There
> are seldom enough counselors to meet the demand, the majority are
> employed on a part-time basis and have little or no training in working

with adults, and the common practice of holding classes at decentralized sites makes it difficult to organize and deploy counseling personnel effectively.

It is truly unfortunate that counseling services for adults in public schools have not received greater priority, because the need for these services is clear (Goldberg, 1980). This chapter describes how, in the face of diminishing financial resources and programs, counseling services are still provided for adult learners in public schools. Adult counseling programs in Indiana public schools are used as examples.

The Problem

Adult educators in public school settings have long known about the counseling needs of adult learners. They recognize that undereducated adults present a myriad of support service needs that must be met before these clients can fully benefit from educational and career opportunities. The most prevalent problem in Indiana has been insufficient financial resources to address the unique problems of service delivery that exist in most communities. Services are too often unavailable or inaccessible. Because public funds for adult education have not increased at the same rate as the demand for services, funding preference has been given to requests for instructional personnel, books, and administrative services. An assessment of counseling needs conducted by the Indiana Department of Public Instruction (Miller, 1977) revealed that there were very few counselors employed in programs of basic and secondary adult education in the state. Most of those who were employed served the program on a part-time basis. According to the assessment, most counseling functions were being performed by teachers as problems arose in the classroom, and most of counseling involved the students' academic progress. An outside evaluation of the statewide program (Kreitlow, 1972) had revealed a similar finding and questioned the adequacy of the teacher as counselor.

Counseling services may be available, but the personnel involved are sometimes unable to address the specific needs of the clients. This can happen when the type of counseling support needed by clients exceeds the expertise or time of the counselor. It can also happen when clients attend class in the evenings or at a "satellite" location at some distance from a central facility while the counselor works days at the central location. It can even happen because there has been insufficient outreach by counselors, such as interacting with students and teachers in the classroom or during breaks in order to establish rapport and credibility.

Some Solutions

A number of strategies and practices have been devised by practitioners in Indiana programs in order to improve service delivery to adults in the public schools. The Bartholomew Consolidated School Corporation in Columbus, Indiana, provides an example of a large comprehensive program that has resolved some of the problems of diverse client need and classroom accessibility. A number of interagency linkages have been established throughout the state to combat the scarcity of counseling resources. Finally, several approaches are being used effectively to strengthen classroom-based counseling.

Comprehensive Counseling Services. A school district that has managed to establish effective counseling services to meet adult needs is the Bartholomew Consolidated School Corporation, located in Columbus, Indiana, a medium-sized city with a population of approximately 30,000. The adult education program in Columbus includes basic, secondary, and vocational education components. One full-time counselor works at the Day Adult High School and a second full-time counselor works with the night program. Another full-time staff member has the responsibility of spending a portion of her time counseling, working in liaison activities with community agencies, and coordinating the activities of the program advisory committee.

The full-time counselors provide direct one-to-one counseling for personal and family problems as well as for academic and career-related concerns. The counselor/student relationship is facilitated through scheduled meetings during the initial enrollment registration. During such meetings, the counselor helps orient the adult student and explains the services available to help the student with academic, personal, and vocational concerns. The counselor is available during school hours, and students may drop in whenever they feel the need. Such an initial meeting is felt to be very important in helping students·feel welcome and know that someone cares about their educational experience.

The counselor also plays a major role in making appropriate referrals and in working with groups and organizations that can assist adult students. A high priority, for example, is placed on securing financial assistance to enable adult students to complete high school and to go on to higher education. Through a trust fund handled by the Bartholomew School Board Foundation, students are eligible for financial assistance. However, financial assistance may also take the form of subsidies for transportation or clothing as well as tuition grants or scholarships. Referrals to outside agencies are often made to deal with special student problems. The local community mental health center, a treatment center for chemical dependency, the welfare department, and the family services agency are the most frequently used outside agencies. Because alcohol and drug abuse is a current program priority area, staff members have had intensive training in this area. For example, staff members were sent to an intensive drug workshop in Minneapolis to become familiar with ways of dealing with drug and alcohol concerns. Support groups are now being arranged for persons who have chemical dependency problems.

The counselor also works with teachers in helping to deal with adult student problems, accepting referrals from teachers, and participating in conferences with both students and teachers. One particular area that counselors and teachers work on jointly is student attendance. Follow-up calls are made by the counselor to student absentees. A special class established for potential dropouts operates using a survival skills curriculum. The students may be former dropouts or students who have demonstrated inability to stay in school consistently. The class stresses essentials such as how to study, basic economic skills, and skills for everyday living. This cooperative effort between counselor and teaching staff had a 90 percent success rate in keeping students in school.

Interagency Linkages. Adult program administrators in the public school often assume that for a student counseling service to be generally available to adult clients it must be provided solely through the public school program. In contrast, as a consequence of limited resources, 40 percent of the Adult Basic Education (ABE) programs in Indiana are now making significant use of other community agencies to provide counseling services to its students. In a number of circumstances, these services are available only to certain segments of a program's clientele, for example, only Comprehensive Employment and Training Act (CETA) clients, welfare clients, or vocational rehabilitation clients. Apparently, a greater proportion of the client population seems to be served in programs using this approach than in those where counselors are employed by the school system.

The concept of linkage has received attention in the adult counseling literature (Comly, 1975; Goldberg, 1980; Heffernan, Macy, and Vickers, 1976; Herr and Whitson, 1979; Schlossberg, 1975). There is an obvious advantage to a program that is able to provide services without having to make a significant commitment of its own funds. Adult basic education programs are in a unique position to accomplish this because they serve the same priority target population (primarily unemployed, poor, or handicapped persons) as many other public social service and welfare programs. Agencies are often willing to provide one service in order to avail themselves of another in return. In some instances, the social service agency personnel have initiated the contact. Agencies providing job training and placement under CETA have found that many clients need basic skill development as a prerequisite. CETA sponsors employ counselors who recruit the client, diagnose employment and training goals, assess entry skill levels, assist the student to develop a personal educational plan, and work directly with teachers in the adult basic education program to develop the educational program. The counselors also follow up to assess the long-range impact of education and training.

In at least two instances in Indiana, the CETA program pays the salaries of counseling personnel who are assigned full-time to the adult education program. In Pike County, Indiana, a rural area in southern Indiana, a counselor is employed by CETA simply because of the great number of clients being served. Part-time counseling services previously provided by the Pike schools were discontinued. In Michigan City, an urban area in northern Indiana, CETA provides a full-time diagnostician to the adult basic education program. She does the intake, goal setting, testing, test interpretation, and follow-up.

One common practice that has led to utilization of agency services by public school adult basic education students has been to establish a classroom site within the facility of the client agency. The school district pays the teacher salaries, while the agency furnishes a room. The agency refers or assigns its clients to the educational program and extends its support service resources to the adult basic education students—in many instances, even to those who are not direct clients of the service agency. In Evansville, Indiana, a major urban center, three adult basic education classes are held at the Area Industrial Institute. The institute has recently made its vocational counseling personnel available to any students enrolled in those classes.

Most of the program administrators who have developed successful interagency service linkages perform the role of a "service broker" in the community. In Gary, Indiana, the adult basic education administrator serves as a member of a city-wide coordinating council. In other areas, program advisory committees comprise social service representatives. In some instances, the administrator actually makes the referral of a student based upon a teacher's recommendation. Since program administrators have long regarded publicity and public relations as part of their jobs, the identification and exchange of service information has been a logical extension of that role.

An example of an adult basic education administrator playing an active role in service linkage with multiple agencies is at Tippecanoe School Corporation near Lafayette, Indiana. Agencies utilized include Employment Security for vocational testing and placement; Rehabilitation Services for vocational counseling and job training; New Directions for assistance to alcohol and drug users; Catholic Charities for assistance to refugees, including job placement; Family Services Agency for psychological problems; and Wabash Valley Mental Health for personal counseling.

Classroom Counseling. The idea, and practice, of teachers performing counseling functions has occasionally been criticized, but if counselors can serve as consultants to teachers and help them acquire some counseling skills, teachers can help provide counseling assistance (Kurpius, 1978). In fact, a modular instructional system is available to help a team involving adult educators and counselors, including instructors and paraprofessionals, to gain confidence for any given counselor skill (Northwest Regional Educational Laboratory, 1975).

Two programs in Indiana developed and demonstrated strategies for strengthening the utilization of the classroom for counseling purposes. At the Blue River Vocational School in Shelbyville, a small town with rural satellite centers, teachers have been involved in a staff development program designed both to improve counseling skills and infuse the curriculum with information to assist students. In addition, through a cooperative arrangement with the area mental health center, the teaching staff participated in six two-and-one-half-hour in-service sessions on listening and responding skills, as well as making referrals. The in-service program continues, and teachers are able to facilitate responses to student concerns or to make appropriate referrals. The Blue

River Adult Education Program also utilizes the vocational school's counselor for vocational interest and aptitude testing, as well as the school district's special education staff for psychometric services. The nature of the program, with its multiple sites separated by great distances, dictates that teachers perform a great deal of academic and personal counseling. The program curriculum also incorporates material designed to help students develop problem-solving skills and to deal with their roles as spouses, parents, consumers, and citizens.

The Southeastern Area Vocational School in Versailles, Indiana, takes another approach to infusing counseling-related services into the curriculum. At Southeastern, student activities are modeled after a special project, *Focus on Choice* (Miller and Pugh, 1979), on the use of group techniques for personal development, goal setting, and problem solving. The project, conducted through the Fort Wayne Women's Bureau, developed a variety of techniques and materials. Southeastern has adopted the approach by using regular class time for these activities on a periodic basis. The activities include decision making and drawing up a personal action plan concerning one's life or career. The program was initially started in the vocational school but is now conducted by the area mental health center. The format usually involves two-hour sessions. The first hour features someone from the community who discusses certain topics such as home repair, credit and banking, insurance, and a variety of life skills. The second hour is devoted to decision making and personal action planning. The program has provided students with counseling and support services in the classroom and has served to successfully meet specific needs of the adult learner.

Summary

It is clear that adult learners in the public school setting — whether they be ABE, general educational diploma, secondary, or vocational students — have counseling needs. Financial limitations and program restrictions frequently make it difficult for these needs to be met. Providing in-house counselors for adult learners can be very beneficial to the educational program. Yet the limitations mentioned earlier apparently prohibit the widespread provision of such assistance. In view of such limitations, linkages between the public school adult programs and community agencies can serve to meet the needs of adult learners. Counselors working with the classroom teacher offer another approach to extending limited counseling resources for adult learning. In-service education to help teachers learn basic counseling concepts such as listening and referral skills and to help them incorporate ideas and practices into the curriculum can also serve to extend counseling services to adult learners.

References

Comly, L. *Community-Based Educational and Career Information and Counseling Services for the Adult Public.* Draft report. Albany: New York State Education Department, 1975.

Darkenwald, G. G. "Educational and Career Guidance for Adults: Delivery System Alternatives." *The Vocational Guidance Quarterly,* 1980, *28* (2), 200–207.

Goldberg, J. C. "Counseling the Adult Learner: A Selective Review of the Literature." *Adult Education,* 1980, *30* (2), 67–81.

Heffernan, J., Macy, F., and Vickers, D. *Educational Brokering: A New Service for Adult Learners.* Syracuse, N.Y.: National Center for Educational Brokering, 1976.

Herr, E. L., and Whitson, K. S. "Career Guidance of Urban Adults: Some Perspectives on Needs and Action." *The Vocational Guidance Quarterly,* 1979, *28* (2), 111–120.

Kreitlow, B. *Indiana Adult Basic Education: An Improvement Evaluation.* Indianapolis: Division of Adult and Community Education, Indiana Department of Public Instruction, 1972.

Kurpius, D. (Ed.). "Consultation, I and II." *Personnel and Guidance Journal,* 1978, *56* (6, 7).

Miller, H., and Pugh, M. *Final Report of Adult Education's Staff Training Program: Focus on Choice.* Indianapolis: Division of Adult and Community Education, Indiana Department of Public Instruction, 1979.

Miller, J. D. *An Indiana Assessment: Counseling Needs of Adults in Adult Basic Education Programs.* Indianapolis: Division of Adult and Community Education, Indiana Department of Public Instruction, 1977.

Northwest Regional Educational Laboratory. *Skills for Adult Guidance Educators.* Portland, Ore.: Northwest Regional Educational Laboratory, 1975.

Schlossberg, N. K. "Programs for Adults." *Personnel and Guidance Journal,* 1975, *53* (9), 681–685.

Frank R. DiSilvestro is assistant professor of the School of Continuing Studies, Indiana University, Bloomington.

Mary Grcich Williams is director, Division of Adult and Community Education, Indiana Department of Public Instruction.

Successful career guidance services for adults currently exist,
but exciting technological innovations will be able to assist
future guidance efforts.

Current and Future
Delivery Systems for
Adult Career Guidance

Solomon Arbeiter

There are a variety of theories to guide career counselors as they seek to determine client service needs. The concept of developmental stages has recently been popularized by Sheehy (1976) and academically supported in works by Levinson and others (1978) and Stevenson (1977). This school describes an evolution of adult needs with increasing age, generally attributing changing characteristics to stages in development. Early, middle, and late adulthood are equated with different levels of adult activity — different career outlooks and needs. Neugarten (1968) and, to a lesser degree, Lowenthal and Weiss (1976) move away from age-related characteristics and posit a richer and more complex series of factors that influence adult perceptions. Social factors such as work relationships and family cohesion are added to the chronological stages as adult motivators. Of direct application to career needs, Arbeiter (1979) posited that the "stage of readiness" for a career transition was critical in selecting the type of career guidance materials and processes required by adults.

What becomes clear is that the institution or individual wishing to offer career guidance services is faced with a bewildering array of adult characteristics and traits to be assessed prior to providing appropriate counseling. The complexity of matching individual characteristics with guidance needs can be illustrated by developing a matrix (Arbeiter, 1979). Individual characteristics, such as age, life cycle stage, employment level, educational level, family status, and additional characteristics could be matched with guidance needs, such as self-awareness, career awareness, social awareness, work effectiveness, skill awareness, decision making, and additional needs. The cross cutting of characteristics with needs has illustrated that clients usually require assistance in two or three different areas. Career guidance agencies currently handle this multiplicity of needs and treatments in several ways.

Current Programs

Many counseling centers and services manage the complexity by limiting their clients to particular age, sex, or educational levels, and they do not attempt to meet all the guidance needs of their clients. For example, one of the better-known and more effective career guidance services is operated by Catalyst. Catalyst is a counseling program housed in New York City and is targeted toward female clients in several of the sites, particularly toward women in mid-life seeking to change careers or to make the transition from homemaker to employee. This focus on a single major client group with a narrow range of concerns — career guidance rather than alcoholism, for example — makes eminently good sense. There is a discrete limit to the number of connections a counselor can make between client needs and available resources and, as information sources appear to be expanding steadily, it is the client pool that can most readily be limited.

CETA Counseling. This process is followed by many of the major career guidance projects. Norman Kurland, director of Adult Learning Services for New York State, has observed that the Comprehensive Employment Training Act (CETA) training centers in New York comprise one of the largest career counseling operations in the state. Each training center offers some form of counseling and career guidance that matches the aspirations and abilities of clients with available training opportunities and jobs. By law, the CETA clients must be unemployed or underemployed, and with a continuous shortage of funds and training slots unemployed individuals constitute the bulk of CETA trainees. Accordingly, the range of counselor concerns narrow to those of career guidance and initial employment, which may be more urgent than longer-term job progression. The client is similarly motivated in that he or she is normally referred to a CETA training center after a period of unemployment and is anxious and willing to be guided to areas with immediate job potential. The information base to be developed by the CETA counselor is therefore focused strongly upon local job requirements and industry needs. With this knowledge base, the counselor can offer the most practical and useful information and direction to the CETA client.

Educational Brokering. The brokering centers established in Syracuse, New York, in the early seventies, and now operating in most parts of the United States through the efforts of the National Center for Educational Brokering, offer a slightly modified variation on the career theme. The goal of the brokering effort is to act as an honest negotiator between the individual in search of an initial career or a career change and the variety of educational institutions that offer training, credentials, and certification toward careers. The brokering agency intends to evaluate the individual's career aspirations and select the most appropriate educational institution to meet the career development needs. The underlying assumption is that the counseling services operated by schools and colleges would be biased toward the educational offerings of the particular institution providing the guidance service, and that the role of an impartial broker would be important.

The brokering agencies, therefore, while receptive to a broad array of clients and client needs, limit the variety of information on hand to the educational offerings of schools, colleges, and other agencies within a specified geographical area. This simplifies the data collection needs of the counselor and minimizes the updating of factual material, such as the schedule of course offerings at institutions, the cost of these offerings, and the changing requirements for certification. Many brokering operations are maintained by a single professional staff person, who established a close relationship with the client. With some financial support from community organizations or concerned state agencies, a brokering agency can charge a minimal fee and offer educational guidance to a diverse clientele seeking career change through education.

Career Education Delivery Systems. An alternative process for limiting client diversity might best be labeled "serendipity." That is, a particular center or service seeks a broad clientele but, through a combination of location, staff interest, or service delivery system, quite rapidly finds that a majority of its clients have similar characteristics and needs. A good example would be the Career Education Project (CEP), which operated in Providence, Rhode Island, for a three-year period in the early seventies. CEP was one of four career education delivery systems supported by the federal government (home-, school-, work-, and center-based). CEP, the home-based model, delivered guidance and counseling services over the telephone to interested clientele in and around Providence. No fee was charged for the service, and telephone counseling enabled clients to call in, or be called, in their home and at a time convenient to them.

What rapidly developed, however, was that the clientele became overwhelmingly female (approximately 80 percent) and younger (approximately 35 years of age) with primary interest in moving from homemaker to employee (Arbeiter and others, 1978). Many women whose children had passed the infant and toddler stages, women who were responding to the emerging women's liberation movement, saw in CEP a way to obtain advice, counseling, and specific educational and career information without leaving the initial security of their home environment. In a move to attract men, the project placed an advertisement for clients during the televised broadcast of the Superbowl. Although this led to an initial influx of male clients, it was of short duration and women continued as the basic constituency.

This narrowed clientele simplified the guidance process for CEP professional and paraprofessional staff, and they concentrated their efforts on obtaining data and information for initial job entry or reentry for women in mid-life. The basic result of this emphasis was a concentration on educational offerings in and around the Providence area and an orientation toward advising clients who had been homemakers for at least a decade as to the advantages of returning to school or college prior to entering a job or career. The result of this effort was a clientele where a strikingly high 85 percent of clients undertook some relevant action subsequent to counseling and, of that number, more than half entered an educational program as part of a transition to job or career.

A simple variation on the theme of limiting client types, either by intent or custom, is to assign particular staff to certain clientele. In one career counseling center in New York City operated by the YMCA, there were three professional staff, all with long experience and detailed knowledge of the counseling process. The clients at the center represented a broad variety of urban residents: highly credentialed younger women serving as secretaries, middle-aged business people and professionals seeking new challenges and new careers, minority group members working in lower-middle–level capacities seeking broader challenges and greater income, and so forth. What became evident as the discussion and interviews progressed was that the clientele were grouped by type and, as early as the initial intake interview, were assigned to a particular counselor who had developed some expertise and knowledge within that area. For example, mid-career business people seeking reorientation to enable them to "operate motels or ski chalets" became the special province of one of the professionals. For the most part, the advice to them was to remain within their profession (which, by the time of mid-life, paid higher salaries than could be obtained elsewhere) and seek to explore and fulfill other career needs through avocational pursuits. An attorney with a brokerage firm, for example, was urged to set up a woodworking shop in his garage or basement and seek to build finely crafted furniture as opposed to opening a carpentry shop or furniture-making business. In this way, through assignment of particular clientele to staff experienced with their needs, the counseling center simplified the matching of client needs to the broad spectrum of career scenarios.

The Typical Assessment Process

There is much less variation in the client needs assessment and career guidance process than there is in categorization of clients for service delivery. The assignment process normally consists of an initial intake interview to obtain basic demographic data from the client and to make basic inquiries as to career, job, and life goals. In most centers, this interview is conducted by a professional staff person, although in some large guidance programs (particularly public programs such as those operated by state employment services) this step may be performed by a trained paraprofessional.

In many instances, the client is then administered a series of short diagnostic instruments to assess career and job aptitudes and interests, for example, Holland's Self-Directed Search and Kuder Preference, and perhaps an instrument such as the Tests of Adult Basic Education to obtain some baseline indications of verbal and mathematical ability. After completing such tests, the client is often given an assignment or task to be performed prior to the next in-person interview. The task varies with the individual. For example, many women seeking to move to the world of work from the role of homemaker are asked to prepare a résumé listing the skills and experiences they have obtained while serving as volunteer workers, PTA president, political party activist, club officer, and so forth. Individuals with a work history may be asked to explore career and job descriptions contained in the *Dictionary of Occupational Titles* or to review one of the many books on career change. Assigning some work to the clients has the effect of involving them more closely in the counseling process and contributes to the feeling that they have control over their future.

The second interview normally takes place approximately two weeks after the intake interview and assessment. This gives the client an opportunity to complete any work he or she was asked to undertake and permits the counselor to review the test results and develop some suggestions for future activity or exploration. The client and counselor briefly discuss the test scores within the context of specific career opportunities or jobs that have been uncovered by either client or the counselor. It is rare for a guidance service to make specific job referrals; rather, the counselor will suggest types of businesses or industries that the client might investigate and specific search agencies or employment agencies are recommended as having had success in placement within particular industries.

The client is then given an appointment approximately six weeks in the future. The basic purpose of the third, and often concluding, guidance session is to enable the client and the counselor to evaluate progress made to date in locating specific industries and businesses and in obtaining job interviews or informational interviews with personnel directors or program managers. The counselor recommends future steps and offers a reinforcement of client action to date.

A Future Scenario

The role of the career counselor can be viewed as that of a middleman. He or she sits at the nexus where the spectrum of client needs and aspirations meets the available data, information, and future activities. Traditionally, the career counselor negotiates the "best fit" between client abilities and aspirations and available jobs or potential careers.

However, another scenario is emerging, one that offers a more useful and humane role for the career counselor. The use of interactive computer programs, view screen terminals, videotapes, and video discs is becoming more widespread. This technology, which can be utilized by the client at a time and place of his or her choosing, is steadily decreasing in cost and, therefore, continually increasing in availability. It increases the self-reliance of the client in that he or she can select among a greater number of variables without needing the benign guidance of the counselor. To the extent that career guidance software packages increase in number and improve in quality, the resources available to the client through a counseling service with this equipment become infinitely greater and offer increased options for client review.

A scenario for a future career counseling service might be as follows. The client arrives at a scheduled time, is asked to pay a fee, and is ushered in to a room with a computer terminal. When the client presses the "on" button, the machine lights up and offers a warm greeting. In the following conversation with the machine, the client is led through a series of questions and assessments that continually narrows the options of career fields, jobs, and educational specifications required for these careers and jobs. The final result, placed on hard copy by pressing a button on the terminal, consists of: (1) instructions for additional reading or activity; (2) a list of careers that serve as a match to the aspirations, interests, and abilities of the client; and (3) recommendations to view a series of prepackaged videotapes or video discs containing job descriptors for particular careers and on-site demonstrations of individuals working in those jobs and performing job-related tasks.

The client is then essentially given a debriefing by the counselor—a dialogue that reviews the process and the outcome of the interaction with the computer. As the client has personally selected the options, the results do not become a matter for debate or disillusionment, and the counseling process can focus on future activities and career searches. The counselor assumes the role of guide rather than middleman. The clients self-select their own scenarios and do not have to be prescreened or assigned to particular counselors. In a similar manner, the computer analyzes and diagnoses the client's needs and their connection to career information and specific jobs, which removes this burden from the counselor. The counselor is able to serve in a supportive and motivational role, and additional sessions can be devoted to an evaluation of client activity.

In many respects, with the possible exception of the broad variety and amount of software, the future is already with us. The Career Information System (CIS) in Oregon (currently being replicated in many states through the support of the National Occupational Information Coordinating Council) has many of the characteristics of the system just described. The element lacking in many cases is concluding sessions with a counselor or a facilitator for encouragement and follow-up.

A series of videotapes and video discs illustrating and illuminating the content of jobs and careers is also needed. Much of this material is in written form from trade associations and is not a satisfactory substitute for viewing machinists, health technicians, computer programmers, or airline clerks performing their daily tasks. The viewing of videotapes comes as close to on-the-job training or site visits as the time and money of the clients and services will allow. As the cost of preparing tapes and discs declines, and the hardware to display this material becomes more readily available, this computer/viewing process will become a significant component of the career counseling service.

References

Arbeiter, S. "Barriers and Facilitators Influencing Participation in Adult Career Guidance Programs." In R. E. Campbell and P. Shaltry (Eds.)., *Perspectives on Adult Career Development and Guidance.* Columbus, Ohio: National Center for Research in Vocational Education, 1979.

Arbeiter, S., and others. *Telephone Counseling for Home-Based Adults.* New York: College Board, 1978.

Levinson, D., and others. *The Seasons of a Man's Life.* New York: Knopf, 1978.

Lowenthal, M. F., and Weiss, L. "Intimacy and Crises in Adulthood." *The Counseling Psychologist,* 1976, *6* (1), 10–15.

Neugarten, B. L. *Middle Age and Aging.* Chicago: University of Chicago Press, 1968.

Sheehy, G. *Passages: Predictable Crises of Adult Life.* New York: Dutton, 1976.

Stevenson, J. L. *Issues and Crises During Middlescence.* New York: Appleton-Century-Crofts, 1977.

Solomon Arbeiter is a planning officer with the College Board in New York City. He has conducted research in the areas of employee training and adult guidance.

*The computer is a viable tool for the delivery of career information
and services to adult learners.*

Computer-Assisted Career Guidance for Adults

Jack R. Rayman

As the ranks of our nation's colleges and universities have swelled with nontraditional learners, educators have increasingly recognized the need for improved
and alternative career-guidance delivery systems. This chapter points out
some of the unique and not-so-unique career development needs of adult populations, briefly describes how one computerized system (DISCOVER) can
help adults meet some of those needs, and identifies other computerized career
guidance systems now under development for adult learners.

    Most career development theorists have concluded that career choice is
an ongoing, lifelong process. Real-life manifestations of this are present all
around us. More and more people are changing their careers in mid-life, women
are reentering the job market in increasing numbers, and workers are often
faced with the stark reality that there is no longer a need for their skills. People
seldom make explicit, systematic choices about how to spend their working
lives. Decision by default is the norm rather than the exception because people
have not learned how to make and implement career-relevant decisions (Thoreson and Ewart, 1976).

    Many of the behaviors traditionally associated with the exploration and
early establishment stages of career development (ages fifteen to forty-five) as
defined by Super (1957) are now recognized as important concerns throughout mid-life. During these stages, individuals move from an awareness of the
need to specify a vocational preference to the execution and completion of def-

inite plans to enter a specific occupation and finally to the search for an entry-level job (Super and others, 1963). At the same time, they must continue to think about their choice of an occupation in terms of a particular life-style, which includes their family life, economic responsibility, leisure-time activities, role in the community, and other factors (Super, 1975b).

The rapidly expanding population of adult learners has thrust new problems upon career counselors and educators. These adult learners are men and women at mid-career shifts — returning veterans, dropouts, women reentering the labor market, military retirees, and career changers. All need information about the availability of educational and occupational opportunities, and many are uncertain about where to seek that information. Adult learners often experience unique problems that are not shared by traditional eighteen-to twenty-one-year-old college students. Examples of these unique problems are:

- Older students may be limited to certain groups of occupations because their need for remedial course work has not been recognized (Lunneborg, Olch, and deWolf, 1974).
- Adult students are at a disadvantage because many counselors have age biases or do not understand the special concerns of older students (Troll and Nowak, 1976).
- Many older students lack confidence in their study skills (Astin, 1976).
- Most existing career development materials and services have been tailored to the needs of traditional college-age students.
- Many adult learners do not have access to on-campus service agencies or to career-related information that frequently travels through the "on-campus pipeline."

Schlossberg (1975) concludes that large numbers of adults are forced to make important career decisions in a vacuum, without the kind of help they desperately require. The evidence suggests that adult learners, more than any other age group, want and need more comprehensive assistance related to career development.

Career Development Theory Applied to Adult Learners

Super's (1975a) definition of "career" is the sequence of positions a person holds throughout his or her preoccupational, occupational, and postoccupational life, including the roles of child, student, worker, spouse, homemaker, parent, user of leisure, citizen, annuitant, and patient.

Walz and Benjamin (1974) also believe that career development should be concerned with the total individual and should encompass education, occupation, and leisure time. They believe career decisions and plans are, in reality, life decisions and plans. Life and career should not be considered separately but as an integrated developmental sequence involving the goals, values, plans, and decisions of the individual now and in the future. Unfortunately, decisions regarding types of schools and colleges and the offerings within them, occupations, and life-styles are often made with limited information or under pressing time constraints (Walz, 1975).

In developmental career theory, the concept of a "life career" suggests that the counseling process should provide individuals with skills and knowledge that have lifelong usefulness. Crites (1976) points out that skills acquired in vocational counseling can be applied to problem solving in other areas at other times in life. Since the choice process is emphasized in developmental and behavioral career counseling, clients have an excellent opportunity to learn important decision-making skills.

David Tiedeman has consistently emphasized the importance of decision making in the career development process. Tiedeman and O'Hara (1963) have divided the process of decision making into two stages, each comprising several phases that lead to the making and implementing of the decision. This model, as elaborated by Miller and Tiedeman (1972), provides a conceptual guide for devising specific counseling strategies to aid the individual in furthering his or her progress and permits counselors to follow the decision-making process in career development programs. One criterion of vocational counseling success might be evidence that students are able to cope with new decision problems (Krumboltz, 1976).

Antecedent to career decision making is the emergence of career awareness — the inventory of knowledge, values, preferences, and self-concepts that an individual draws on in the course of making career choices (Wise, Tharner, and Randour, 1976). If the career development process is closely related to self-concept clarification (Super and others, 1963), one of the vocational behaviors at the clarification stage is that individuals are able to express career-relevant characteristics (needs, values, aptitudes, vocational interests, and vocational aspirations) about themselves (Thoni and Olsson, 1975). A comprehensive career development program should therefore include learning experiences that help to develop career awareness. A few programs currently being used with college and adult students emphasize the importance of raising career awareness (Chapman, Norris, and Katz, 1973; Figler, 1975; Walz, 1975; Rayman, 1978a).

If sound career decisions are to result from the effects of a program, that program should be developed with sensitivity to social, cultural, economic, and political conditions that influence career decisions. Where possible, the freedom of the decision maker should be increased by helping the individual to be aware of the constraints and by teaching ways to function effectively in spite of them (Jones and Jung, 1976).

The Computer as a Delivery System

The rapid development of computer technology has created interest in the potential of computers to assist in the delivery of career guidance (Harris, 1974). Campbell (1974) feels that guidance often falls victim to routine and obsolete practices. He believes an emerging trend that will enhance career development is the use of the computer as a delivery system. Harrison and Entine (1976) and Farmer (1976) support this view and point out that computer delivery systems have the potential for expanding guidance programs to meet the needs of adult populations.

Holland (1976) believes that reasonably successful computer-assisted forms of vocational guidance have already been demonstrated. One virtue of this delivery method is in the presentation of standard treatment modules that, if carefully written, can eliminate even the most subtle kinds of bias and can have considerable potential for research into the vocational treatment process.

Harris-Bowlsby (1975) has outlined the status and success of seven existing computer-based career guidance systems. Although such systems are not in wide use, successes have been achieved with high school and college students and adults in a community setting. Field evaluation has shown that use of the Computerized Vocational Information System (CVIS) with high school students (Harris, 1972) causes a significant increase in the range and accuracy of information possessed about specific occupations. CVIS is a computerized system designed primarily for the rapid storage and retrieval of occupational information for use in high school guidance programs. The same conclusion is supported by data from the field trial of the Education and Career Exploration System — one of the earliest computerized career guidance systems designed for use at the high school level (Thompson and others, 1970).

The System for Interactive Guidance Information (SIGI), though designed for use with college students, has also been used with some success by adult learners. In Oregon, use of the Computerized Information System (McKinlay and Franklin, 1975) in community colleges, shopping centers, and a correctional institution has helped adult learners to increase knowledge about their first-choice occupation and caused them to think more carefully about vocational and educational plans.

One of the more recent computer-based career guidance programs, called DISCOVER (Bowlsbey and Rayman, 1975), is a comprehensive program designed to enhance normal career development for seventh through twelfth grades. Analyses of DISCOVER field trial data show that users are able to make progress toward specifying both educational and vocational goals in a short time, that they view their overall experience in very positive terms, and that they find computer-delivered values clarification and decision-making materials to be helpful (Bowlsbey, Rayman, and Bryson, 1976). These findings led to the development of a college/adult version of the DISCOVER system.

Through the financial support of the Exxon Education Foundation, Rayman (1978b) directed the adaptation of the DISCOVER Computerized Career Guidance System for college students and adults. This adult-level system represents an attempt to combine current career development theory with the unique delivery capabilities of the computer. A number of capabilities of the computer make it a particularly valuable tool for delivering career information and services to adults. It can:

- store, search, retrieve, relate, and update large data files with ease and accuracy
- interrelate computer-stored data about a user with data about schools and occupations in a way that creates new information for the user
- simulate structured interviews with a high degree of personalization through the use of cathode ray terminals with light pens
- provide individualized attention to many users at multiple remote locations simultaneously for many hours per day
- monitor a user's progress in career decision making and provide appropriate feedback, clarification, or review.

Further evidence in support of using the computer in the delivery of career services stems from the evaluation of its effectiveness in currently operational systems at the high school and college levels (Bowlsbey, Rayman, and Bryson, 1976; Chapman, Norris, and Katz, 1973; Harris, 1972; Impelleteri, 1968; Maola, 1974; Melhus, 1971; Myers and others, 1972; Price, 1971; Rayman, 1978a; Rayman, Bryson, and Bowlsbey, 1978). A summary of the evaluation of existing computer-based systems indicates that:

- They are enthusiastically accepted and easily used by students.
- They cause an increase in conversation about career planning.
- They cause measured increases in vocational maturity, occupational exploration, occupational knowledge, self-knowledge, and specification of career plans.
- Individuals prefer to get career information from a computer rather than from books, files, and other traditional sources.
- Some career guidance functions can be done as well by computer as by counselors, at a lower per-hour cost.
- The computer is perceived by many users as a less threatening and less biased purveyor of career information than a counselor.

Content of the College/Adult DISCOVER System

DISCOVER is a systematic career development program designed to enhance normal career development for college students and adults. The study of career development theory makes it clear that a career development system should include at least the following components: (1) self-information, including techniques for the identification and clarification of values, interests, transferable skills, and competencies; (2) exploration of occupations in a systematic way; (3) teaching and low-risk practice of career decision making; (4) relationship of self-information to occupational alternatives; and (5) informational assistance with the implementation of a career choice.

DISCOVER provides assistance in all of these areas through twelve fifty-minute modules of interactive content. Some tools and techniques developed and copyrighted by other guidance professionals are used within DISCOVER by permission, and in some cases with royalty agreements. Examples of these are Holland's Self-Directed Search (1972) and Super's Career Decision Tree (1975a). Seven large data files, including 442 occupations, 1400 + four-year colleges, 850 + two-year colleges, 11,000 technical and specialized schools, 400 + military training programs, and 500 + graduate and professional schools, support the users' search for occupational and educational alternatives. In summary, DISCOVER is a combination of originally developed interactive dialogue and simulations, of instruments and tools used by permission of other developers, and of originally developed and borrowed data files.

The "main line" modules of the system are graphically depicted in Figure 1. The position of each module on the arrow-shaped diagram is based on a developmental approach to career guidance. Super's Developmental Stages (1963) and Tiedeman and O'Hara's Decision-Making Paradigm (1963) are plotted at the bottom of the diagram to depict the association that exists between the content of each module and these two developmental theories. In the DISCOVER system, a person of low vocational maturity would be advised to begin with Module 1a (at the left end of the arrow) and to proceed in numerical order through Module 8 and its submodules (at the tip of the arrow). DISCOVER does, however, accommodate individual differences of interest and vocational maturity by allowing the user to enter the system at any point, to use it in any order, or to receive a suggested sequence through the system by taking an instrument called the survey of career development (Rayman and Super, 1975), which is contained in the entry module (an administrative section of the system that orients the user to the system and monitors use). The titles and numbers of each DISCOVER module are presented in Table 1, together with a brief description of the corresponding career guidance content. Detailed descriptions of the content of each module are available in the *DISCOVER College/Adult Professional Manual* (Rayman, 1978b).

Discussion

Experience with existing computerized career development and guidance systems suggests that they possess a number of characteristics that make them particularly appropriate for use with adult populations. Though most of the systems currently in use were not designed specifically for adult populations, considerable evidence has accumulated in support of the efficacy of their use with adult populations. The DISCOVER College/Adult System does incorporate many of the characteristics seen as necessary for adult learners (Rayman, 1977, 1978a, 1978b). Preliminary evaluation of DISCOVER indicates that it is well received and that positive effects are achieved in the areas of increased knowledge of the world of work, increased specificity of career plans, and increased awareness of how to implement career plans (Rayman, 1978a).

The evaluation of DISCOVER with adult populations has led to a better understanding of what career guidance content is best delivered by com-

Figure 1. Diagram of the DISCOVER System

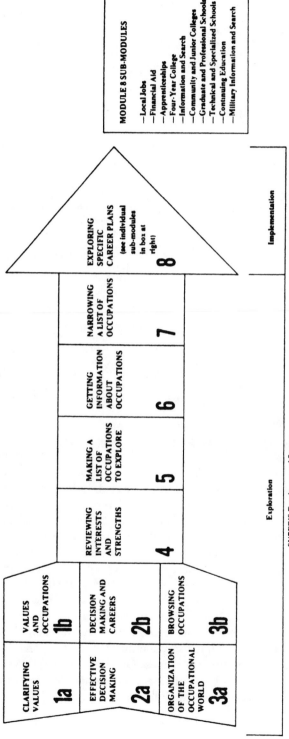

MODULE 8 SUB-MODULES

— Local Jobs
— Financial Aid
— Apprenticeships
— Four-Year College
— Information and Search
— Community and Junior Colleges
— Graduate and Professional Schools
— Technical and Specialized Schools
— Continuing Education
— Military Information and Search

CLARIFYING VALUES	VALUES AND OCCUPATIONS
1a	1b
EFFECTIVE DECISION MAKING	DECISION MAKING AND CAREERS
2a	2b
ORGANIZATION OF THE OCCUPATIONAL WORLD	BROWSING OCCUPATIONS
3a	3b

REVIEWING INTERESTS AND STRENGTHS — 4

MAKING A LIST OF OCCUPATIONS TO EXPLORE — 5

GETTING INFORMATION ABOUT OCCUPATIONS — 6

NARROWING A LIST OF OCCUPATIONS — 7

EXPLORING SPECIFIC CAREER PLANS (see individual sub-modules in box at right) — 8

Exploration

Implementation

SUPER'S Developmental Stages

Crystallization — Choice — Clarification Induction

Anticipation

Exploration — Implementation

TIEDEMAN's Decision-making Paradigm (truncated)

Table 1. DISCOVER Modules Related to Career Guidance Content

Five Components of a Systematic Approach to Adult Career Guidance	Corresponding DISCOVER Modules	User Description of Components
1. Self-information, including techniques	1a, 1b, 4	Getting Information About Yourself
2. Exploration of occupations in a systematic way	2b, 3a, 3b, 5, 6	Getting Information About Occupations
3. Teaching and low-risk practice of career decision making	2a, 2b, 7	Getting Information About Career Decision Making
4. Relationship of self-information to occupational alternatives and reality testing	5, 6, 7, 8	Using What You've Learned About Yourself, Decision Making, and the World of Work to Make a Tentative Career Choice
5. Informational assistance with implementation of career choice	8	Implementing Your Career Plans: Local Jobs Financial Aid Apprenticeships Four-Year College Information and Search Community and Junior Colleges Graduate and Professional Schools Technical and Specialized Schools Continuing Education Military Information and Search Mid-Career Job Changes

puter and what might be more efficiently or powerfully delivered by other, more traditional means. The development of computerized systems continues on several fronts. JoAnn Bowlsbey at Towson State University has drawn on experience with DISCOVER to develop a more streamlined computerized career development system for college students called EXPLORE. The DISCOVER Foundation at Towson State University has recently received a grant from the Council for Advancement of Experiential Learning (CAEL) for the development of a computerized career guidance system designed specifically for use by adult learners. Similarly, the Educational Testing Service has received a Kellogg Foundation grant to evaluate the use of the System for Interactive Guidance Information (SIGI) with adult learners (Norris, 1980). This evaluational effort, entitled "Project LEARN," should result in specific recommendations for the modification of SIGI for use with adult learners.

Clearly, there are many unanswered questions surrounding the use of computers in career guidance. Only time, continued evaluation, and development will provide answers to these questions. One thing seems certain, however: Computers will play an ever increasing role in the delivery of career guidance and career information to adult learners.

References

Astin, H. "Continuing Education and the Development of Adult Women." *Counseling Psychologist,* 1976, *6* (1), 55–60.

Bowlsbey, J. E., and Rayman, J. R. *DISCOVER Professional Manual.* Towson, Md.: DISCOVER Foundation, 1975.

Bowlsbey, J. E., Rayman, J. R., and Bryson, D. L. *DISCOVER Field Trial Report.* Towson, Md.: DISCOVER Foundation, 1976.

Campbell, D. E. "Career Guidance Practices Transcending the Present." *Vocational Guidance Quarterly,* 1974, *22,* 292–300.

Chapman, W., Norris, L., and Katz, M. R. *SIGI: Report of a Pilot Study Under Field Conditions.* Princeton, N.J.: Educational Testing Service, 1973.

Crites, J. O. "Career Counseling: A Comprehensive Approach." *Counseling Psychologist,* 1976, *6* (3), 2–12.

Farmer, H. "INQUIRY Project: Computer-Assisted Counseling Center for Adults." *Counseling Psychologist,* 1976, *6* (1), 50–54.

Figler, H. E. *PATH: A Career Workbook for Liberal Arts Students.* Cranston, R.I.: Carroll Press, 1975.

Harris, J. E. "Analysis of the Effects of a Computer-Based Vocational Information System on Selected Aspects of Vocational Planning." Unpublished doctoral dissertation, Northern Illinois University, 1972.

Harris, J. E. "The Computer: Guidance Tool of the Future." *Journal of Counseling Psychology,* 1974, *21* (4), 331–339.

Harris-Bowlsbey, J. E. *Computers in Guidance: A Status Report.* Unpublished manuscript, Western Maryland College, 1975.

Harrison, L. R., and Entine, A. D. "Existing Programs and Emerging Strategies." *Counseling Psychologist,* 1976, *6* (1), 45–49.

Holland, J. L. *The Self-Directed Search.* Palo Alto, Calif.: Consulting Psychologists Press, 1972.

Holland, J. L. "A New Synthesis for an Old Method and a New Analysis of Some Old Phenomena." *Counseling Psychologist,* 1976, *6* (3), 12–15.

Impelleteri, J. T. *Computer-Assisted Occupational Guidance: The Development and Evaluation of a Pilot Computer-Assisted Occupational Guidance Program.* Final report. University Park: Vocational Education Department, Pennsylvania State University, 1968.

Jones, G., and Jung, M. "Research Priorities and Resources in Career Decision Making." *Counseling Psychologist,* 1976, *6* (3), 43–46.

Krumboltz, J. D. "This Chevrolet Can't Float or Fly." *Counseling Psychologist,* 1976, *6* (3), 17–19.

Lunneborg, W., Olch, D. R., and deWolf, F. "Prediction of College Performance in Older Students." *Journal of Counseling Psychology,* 1974, *21* (3), 215–221.

McKinlay, B., and Franklin, P. L. *Education Components for a Career Information System.* Eugene: University of Oregon, 1975.

Maola, J. F. "An Assessment of Career Information Between OWE Students Using a Counselor-Based vs. Computer-Based Information System." Unpublished doctoral dissertation, University of Akron, 1974.

Melhus, G. E. "Computer-Assisted Vocational Choice Compared with Traditional Vocational Counseling." Unpublished doctoral dissertation, Illinois Institute of Technology, 1971.

Miller, A., and Tiedeman, D. V. *Career Decision Making.* Unpublished manuscript, 1972.

Myers, R., and others. *Educational and Career Exploration System: Report of a Two-Year Trial.* New York: Teachers College, Columbia University, 1972.

Norris, L. *Research Scientist.* Princeton, N.J.: Educational Testing Service, 1980.

Price, G. E. "A Comparison of Computer and Counselor Effectiveness in Assisting

94

High School Students Explore and Select Courses." Unpublished doctoral dissertation, Michigan State University, 1971.

Pyle, K. R., and Stripling, R. O. "The Counselor, the Computer, and Career Development." *The Vocational Guidance Quarterly,* 1976, *25* (1), 71–75.

Rayman, J. R. "DISCOVER: A Computerized Careers Curriculum." In *Proceedings of 1977 Conference on Computers in the Undergraduate Curricula.* East Lansing: Michigan State University, 1977.

Rayman, J. R. *DISCOVER: A College/Adult-Level Computerized Career Guidance and Information System.* Final report. Towson: DISCOVER Foundation, Western Maryland College, 1978a.

Rayman, J. R. *DISCOVER College/Adult Professional Manual.* Towson, Md.: DISCOVER Foundation, 1978b.

Rayman, J. R., Bryson, D. L., and Bowlsbey, J. E. "The Field Trial of DISCOVER: A New Computerized Interactive Guidance System." *Vocational Guidance Quarterly,* 1978, *26* (4), 349–360.

Rayman, J. R., and Super, D. E. *Survey of Career Development.* Instrument developed for use as a part of the DISCOVER System. Towson, Md.: DISCOVER Foundation, 1975.

Schlossberg, N. K. "Programs for Adults." *Personnel and Guidance Journal,* 1975, *53* (9), 681–684.

Super, D. E. *The Psychology of Careers.* New York: Harper & Row, 1957.

Super, D. E. *Career Decision Tree.* New York: Teachers College, Columbia University, 1975a.

Super, D. E. "How People Make and Might Be Helped to Make Career Choices." Paper presented at CRAC/NICEC Seminar, Cambridge, England, King's College, July 1975b.

Super, D. E., and others. *Career Development: Self-Concept Theory.* Research Monograph no. 4. New York: College Entrance Examination Board, 1963.

Thompson, A. S., and others. *The Educational and Career Exploration System: Field Trial and Evaluation in Montclair High School.* New York: Teachers College Press, 1970.

Thoni, R. J., and Olsson, P. M. "A Systematic Career Development Program in a Liberal Arts College." *Personnel and Guidance Journal,* 1975, *53* (9), 672–675.

Thoreson, C. E., and Ewart, K. "Behavioral Self-Control and Career Development." *Counseling Psychologist,* 1976, *6* (3), 29–43.

Tiedeman, D. V., and O'Hara, R. P. *Career Development: Choice and Adjustment.* Research Monograph no. 3. New York: College Entrance Examination Board, 1963.

Troll, E., and Nowak, C. "How Old Are You?—The Question of Age Bias in the Counseling of Adults." *Counseling Psychologist,* 1976, *6* (1), 41–44.

Walz, G. R. "Swinging into the Future." *Personnel and Guidance Journal,* 1975, *53* (9), 712–716.

Walz, G. R., and Benjamin, L. *The Life Career Development System: A Comprehensive View of Career Development.* Washington, D.C.: American Personnel and Guidance Association, 1974.

Wise, R., Tharner, L., and Randour, J. L. "A Conceptual Framework for Career Awareness in Career Decision Making." *Counseling Psychologist,* 1976, *6* (3), 47–53.

Jack R. Rayman is career development and placement officer, College of Sciences and Humanities, and adjunct assistant professor of psychology at Iowa State University. He directed the development of the college/adult version of DISCOVER and is on the Board of Directors of the DISCOVER Foundation.

Now that the counseling needs of nontraditional learners have been recognized, it is time to recognize that nontraditional counseling methods can help meet them.

"The Medium Is . . . ": Nontraditional Approaches to Counseling Adult Learners

Judith B. Wertheim

As this sourcebook indicates, there has been a recent surge of interest in counseling adult learners. Despite this interest, however, the status of adult counseling itself remains unclear. Many authors (Darkenwald, 1980; Farmer, 1971; Harrison, n.d.; Ironside and Jacobs, 1977) lament the current situation, observing that although educational opportunities for adult learners have increased dramatically, counseling opportunities have not similarly increased. Yet some of the same writers (Darkenwald, 1980; Ironside and Jacobs, 1977) proceed to cite ways in which adult learners are currently being counseled. Apparent inconsistencies occur as well when the focus narrows to nontraditional methods of counseling adult learners. Thornton and Mitchell (1978), for example, in a thorough survey of nontraditional methods of counseling adult learners, speak of the dearth of literature about the subject. The same authors, however, then manage to identify 150 instances of nontraditional counseling. Reading this survey, in fact, one is overwhelmed by the number of nontraditional programs available to adult learners.

What, then, is a reasonable assessment of nontraditional counseling for adults? Is there a great deal or too little? There is, paradoxically, both—both a great deal of nontraditional counseling available for adult learners and too little of it. On the one hand, as the following survey will indicate, current uses of media to advise adult learners are extensive. On the other hand, counseling that goes beyond advising is infrequently provided for adult learners.

Uses of Media

Nontraditional counseling for adults can be viewed from at least two perspectives. This type of counseling is often defined in the literature either as that which uses nontraditional methods and does not involve face-to-face communication or as counseling which, though face-to-face, occurs in nontraditional settings. As different as they are in focus or setting, all nontraditional approaches to counseling seek, nonetheless, to help adults who cannot regularly be present at a university, who have otherwise limited access to counseling, or who feel their concerns need immediate attention.

Following is a brief review of some of the ways in which nontraditional forms of counseling are currently used. This review is not meant to be a comprehensive list of all nontraditional counseling programs for adults. Rather, it is an overview of the ways in which the media can be used to help adults and of some of the noninstitutional settings in which adults may be helped. Readers who desire more detailed information about the variety of programs available or about a specific program are referred to Ironside and Jacobs (1977) and Thornton and Mitchell (1978) or to descriptions of the programs themselves.

Written Communication. Correspondence, perhaps one of the most traditional methods of communication, can, ironically, also be a nontraditional method of counseling. Writing to ask advice of peers or professionals on an informal basis may be routine. When, however, correspondence is formalized and involves several exchanges, it is considered innovative. What helps to make written communication innovative is the presentation of a guidance package for the adult learner. Going beyond a letter or two about opportunities available at a particular institution or appropriate courses for the adult learner, innovative counseling by correspondence helps adult learners deal with ongoing processes in their lives. There is, for example, the "Women Returning to Work" program (Harrison and Entine, 1976), in which the skills needed by women reentering the work force are strengthened via exchanges of letters. When participants in this program return one packet of materials to the counseling office, another packet is sent out. Development of a dialogue between counselor and student seems, however, to be minimal.

Another approach to counseling via correspondence that encourages a dialogue is exemplified by the courses in career planning and in decision making offered for credit by Indiana University (O'Neal, 1979a; 1979b). In each of these courses, students of all ages, whether or not they are enrolled at Indiana University, are instructed in specific aspects of career development and decision making. These aspects are presented as individual lessons, in which the student responds to both general and personally relevant questions, mails the responses to a counselor/instructor, and receives a response. Because this counseling process involves more than a single information-giving session, an extended relationship between the counselor and the student can develop. Students can progress through the career decision-making courses at their own pace, with time to articulate, reflect, and do research on their own. In addition, because most of the interaction is written down, students have a record of their own behavior and of a counselor's response. This record can later be used as a reference, should similar opportunities for decision making occur.

Of course, counseling via corresponsence is not a panacea for distance learners. First, writing is a chore that many avoid, particularly those who do not write regularly in their daily lives — in other words, precisely those who may be the potential audience, adults who have been out of school for years. Second, counseling via correspondence may involve ethical problems (Wrenn, personal communication). How can the counselor, for example, be sure that the writer is really the client? Or, lacking many cues available in face-to-face counseling, that the client's perceptions are honest? Or that limitations in writing abilities do not obscure the essence of the client's concerns? Ignoring such ethical issues may lead to dispensing superficial advice, much as syndicated newspaper columnists distribute advice, relevant to all but meaningful to few. Yet, with such caveats in mind, the counselor who wishes to help the distant learner can consider correspondence an effective counseling method.

Telephone Use. In our society, the telephone is certainly another traditional method of communication. Yet the telephone can also be a nontraditional method of counseling adult learners. The simplest form of telephone counseling is the routine, single telephone call in which the student whose question demands an immediate answer calls the counselor for specific information, referral, or advice. Such calls are facilitated by the use of toll-free telephone numbers. Further, if the counselor is identified by name, the student has located a resource at the institution and the communication can continue, either by telephone or in another form. The Open University in England has formalized telephone communication with a "telecard" system by which the student can contact a tutor/counselor at a particular time each week to discuss academic concerns (Thornton and Mitchell, 1978).

Thornton and Mitchell also mention use of a party-line system, involving several students who talk to a counselor during a single session. Although this system combines some of the advantages of a group guidance session and peer interaction with a nontraditional medium, the problem of meeting at a central location remains. One way to circumvent this problem may be the conference call that Thornton and Mitchell also cite.

Finally, the Career Education Project, operating in Providence, Rhode Island, from 1972 until 1975, offered telephone counseling "concerned with the career-related needs of home-based adults . . . 16 years of age or older who were neither working full-time nor attending school full-time" (Arbeiter and others, 1978, p. 8). Adults using this service received career information, guidance, and referral from paraprofessional counselors. Those responding to a follow-up survey indicated greatest satisfaction with the "self-exploration, goal setting, and career decision making" activities of the service (p. 2). Clearly, many of the clients developed rapport with a counselor, since the number of telephone interviews for a single client was found to range from one to more than twenty. Nonetheless, routine termination of counseling services when clients either made or began to implement a decision may have ended the relationship precisely when some users most acutely needed support.

Audio Cassettes. Categories of nontraditional approaches to counseling, like counseling activities, often overlap. Use of the telephone, for example, may involve communication between counselor and clients but may also involve twenty-four–hour access to audiotapes related to counseling or advising issues. Whereas the telephone is the vital medium in both approaches, there is no personal interaction between the tape and the listener in the latter. In a recent report àbout the CounseLine Service at Rutgers University, Sperling (1980) reports that about twenty schools have established an audiotape service briefly addressing a variety of issues and offering a list of related referrals. Currently this service appeals primarily to traditional undergraduates' concerns, such as dating and summer jobs, although tapes relevant to all students, for example, on financial aid and medical information, are also available. The repertoire can certainly be extended to include more of the concerns of adult learners. Although the system provides no opportunity for exchange between counselor and student, the audio-cassette-via-telephone service is readily accessible, inexpensive to use, and free of what may be embarrassing face-to-face contact. For adult learners, it appears to be a comfortable first step in the process of making contact with an institution.

Radio and Television. Other approaches to adult counseling that straddle the territory between routine and innovative include the use of radio and television. Shilling (n.d.), for example, reports that the State University of New York at New Paltz offers a radio program that focuses on educational counseling and an introduction to lifelong learning. Shilling also cites a call-in counseling and life-planning show that appears on public television in New Orleans. Certainly, information about educational opportunities can easily be given to large groups when these mass media are used. Yet here, as with counseling via correspondence, ethical problems may arise. How, for example, is one assured of the good faith of the caller? How does one determine that the caller's presenting problem is the pressing one? In addition, counseling is theoretically most effective when the client feels the need for it. How does the use of mass media ensure that the timing of the presentations will suit individual needs?

Computer-Assisted Counseling. Looking into the future, Walz and Benjamin (1980) anticipate the use not only of audio cassettes but of video cassettes, linked to home computers. Currently, in fact, computers are being used in institutional settings to help adults with educational planning and career choice. There is, for example, the DISCOVER College/Adult System, which addresses career development and emphasizes values, decision making, and the occupational world. Although the final report about this system (Rayman, n.d.) contains many appendices on use of the computer-based guidance system with college-age populations, there is little indication that older adults have access to DISCOVER or find it appropriate for their concerns. Perhaps DISCOVER can be expanded to include nontraditional users and another "final report" issued.

Finally, the System for Interactive Guidance and Information (SIGI) is being adapted by the Educational Testing Service to provide career guidance for "adults who are thinking about entering college or changing careers" ("Notes on . . . Continuing Education," 1980). In addition, SIGI will soon use the computer to evaluate adults' experiential learning.

There is no doubt that computer use for career counseling has definite advantages over many other types of counseling. The amount of data stored and instantaneously retrived is enormous. Nonetheless, one wonders whether the computer actually does teach skills to be used when the computer is not available. And of course, use of DISCOVER or SIGI depends on access to an institution that houses one of the systems. For many adult learners, getting to the place where the computer is located may pose insurmountable problems.

Programmed Self-Instructional Material. Less elaborate than computer programs, but using some of the same principles, are the programmed or self-instructional materials that are related primarily to career choice and decision making. Filmstrip/audio cassette/workbook packages (National Career Consultants, 1980–1981), as well as programmed workbooks (Olympus Publishing, 1977) are available directly from individual publishers. Because many of the programmed series are addressed only to specific subgroups of adults — such as those who are college-educated, adult basic education students, or uncertain résumé writers — the search for appropriate materials can often be a long one (Wertheim, 1980). Yet when applicable program texts are located, adult learners can receive substantial help in articulating their own patterns of behavior and goals that they wish to achieve.

Noninstitutional Settings. Interest in nontraditional approaches to counseling comes largely from an effort to formulate programs that appeal to potential university students. Another way to appeal to these adults is an outreach effort that locates counseling and advising centers in nonuniversity settings. Many centers have moved out into the community and currently operate in storefronts, libraries, and shopping centers (Hitchcock, n.d.; Ironside and Jacobs, 1977). Other centers keep moving, operating from mobile vans (Shaltry, n.d.) that regularly visit a community and provide counseling services to those who cannot come to the university. Vans equipped as resource centers, such as the one used by the Vincennes (Indiana) University adult basic education program, allow adult learners and prospective learners to participate in an extended counseling process, similar to that which is available on the campus. Unfortunately, visits may be infrequent because financial exigencies may restrict trips by the mobile vans to once a month or less.

To Resolve the Paradox

It is apparent from the foregoing summary that many nontraditional approaches have been adapted to appeal to adult learners, particularly those who may enroll or are already enrolled in an organized learning program. There seems to be no shortage of innovative approaches to counseling adult learners. Is there? Close examination of the literature about nontraditional counseling of adult learners shows that counseling does abound in the areas of educational and occupational choice. There is citation after citation, for example, of ways to advise students about course requirements and educational options. Nearly all uses of media have, in fact, been directed toward these two objectives. Yet these are clearly not the only two areas with which adult learners have had difficulties. Educational planning itself, for example, may include areas other than choice of courses. There may be problems with study skills, self-confidence, and unrealistic expectations (Brown, 1971). Currently, these concerns are only minimally addressed by nontraditional counseling methods. In addition, adult learners may have other developmental concerns, among them help with managing personal problems and learning problem-solving techniques (Riggs, 1980; University of Southern California, 1978). Moreover, as Campbell and Cellini (n.d.) point out, there is the need to relate specific concerns of adults to adult life stages and the ramifications of those stages.

Trained counselors are certainly aware of the many issues involved in counseling. Certainly they are aware, too, of the distinction made by Ironside and Jacobs (1977) between counseling and advising. Why, then, is the advice-and information-giving function of counseling so overemphasized in the literature about nontraditional counseling approaches to adult learners? Thompson confirms one reason: "Educational counseling is the functional area in which many counselors of adults have the most knowledge and understanding" (1971, p. 22). In addition, academic advisement is often a pressing concern (Darkenwald, n.d.), since it must conform to a time limit. Advice and information, moreover, are most easily translated into forms of communication in which there is little interpersonal exchange or depth of relationship and which may be disseminated in a single session. Exploration of feelings, however, as well as multiple personal concerns, cannot easily be translated into a generally applicable formula. Ironically, while the range of information offered to adults grows wider, definitions of the counseling process grow narrower.

A challenge to practitioners resounds: Counselors must differentiate between form and content related to nontraditional approaches to counseling adult learners. It then becomes clear that even though packages of guidance services seem to take full advantage of existing technology, the range of available counseling content is limited.

Technology to reach those who cannot attend the university on a regular basis certainly exists. Information packages to reach those learners exist, as well. The content of these packages, however, needs scrutiny, for it currently includes little counseling. Can a dialogue (Baath, 1976), a true counseling relationship, be established at a distance? If adult learners are to be adequately served, the focus must be innovative counseling, rather than innovative delivery systems. Clearly, technical skills are adequate for nontraditional counseling. Are counseling skills equally adequate?

References

Arbeiter, S., and others. *Telephone Counseling for Home-Based Adults.* New York: The College Board, 1978.

Baath, J. D. "How to Optimize the Learning Conditions of Correspondence Education." Paper presented at a European Home Study Council Workshop, Paris, Autumn 1976.

Brown, T. O. "Counseling Adults with Educational Problems." In M. L. Farmer (Ed.), *Counseling Services for Adults in Higher Education.* Metuchen, N.J.: Scarecrow Press, 1971.

Campbell, R. E., and Cellini, J. V. "A Critique of the Current Status of Adult Career Development Theory." In R. E. Campbell and P. Shaltry (Eds.), *Perspectives on Adult Career Development and Guidance.* Columbus, Ohio: National Center for Research in Vocational Education, n.d.

Darkenwald, G. G. "Educational and Career Guidance for Adults: Delivery System Alternatives." *Vocational Guidance Quarterly,* 1980, *28* (2), 200-207.

Darkenwald, G. G. "Career and Educational Guidance for Adults: An Organizational Perspective." In R. E. Campbell and P. Shaltry (Eds.), *Perspectives on Adult Career Development and Guidance.* Columbus, Ohio: National Center for Research in Vocational Education, n.d.

Farmer, M. L. "Counseling Adults Is Different." In M. L. Farmer (Ed.), *Counseling Services for Adults in Higher Education.* Metuchen, N.J.: Scarecrow Press, 1971.

Harrison, L. R. "Meaningful Ways of Analyzing or Grouping Target Populations for Adult Career Guidance." In R. E. Campbell and P. Shaltry (Eds.), *Perspectives on Adult Career Development and Guidance.* Columbus, Ohio: National Center for Research in Vocational Education, n.d.

Harrison, L. R., and Entine, A. D. "Existing Programs and Emerging Strategies." *The Counseling Psychologist,* 1976, *6* (1), 45-49.

Hitchcock, A. A. "Public Policy and Adult Career/Occupational Services." In R. E. Campbell and P. Shaltry (Eds.), *Perspectives on Adult Career Development and Guidance.* Columbus, Ohio: National Center for Research in Vocational Education, n.d.

Ironside, D. J., and Jacobs, D. E. *Trends in Counselling and Information Services for the Adult Learner.* Toronto: Ontario Institute for Studies in Education, 1977.

National Career Consultants. *Fascinating World of Work.* Richardson, Tex.: National Career Consultants, 1980-1981.

"Notes on . . . Continuing Education." *Chronicle of Higher Education,* July 7, 1980, p. 2.

Olympus Publishing. *Career Emphasis Series: A Self-Study Approach to Life/Career Planning.* Salt Lake City: Olympus Publishing, 1977.

O'Neal, R. *A Study Guide for COAS Q294 Basic Career Development.* Bloomington: School of Continuing Studies, Indiana University, 1979a.

O'Neal, R. *A Study Guide for College of Arts and Sciences Q394 Career Decision Making.* Bloomington: School of Continuing Studies, Indiana University, 1979b.

Rayman, J. R. *DISCOVER: A College-Level Computerized Career Guidance and Information System.* Final report, n.p., n.d.

Riggs, J. A. *Advising or Counseling Adults.* Urbana: University of Illinois, 1980.

Shaltry, P. "A Profile of Existing Services." In R. E. Campbell and P. Shaltry (Eds.), *Perspectives on Adult Career Development and Guidance.* Columbus, Ohio: National Center for Research in Vocational Education, n.d.

Shilling, L. M. "Women." In R. E. Campbell and P. Shaltry (Eds.), *Perspectives on Adult Career Development and Guidance.* Columbus, Ohio: National Center for Research in Vocational Education, n.d.

Sperling, A. "When You Need Advice but Can't Wait for an Appointment, Just Pick Up Your Telephone and Dial CounseLine." *Rutgers Alumni Magazine,* 1980, *60* (1), 13-16.

Thompson, C. "The Nature of Adult Students and the Scope of Counseling Services." In M. L. Farmer (Ed.), *Counseling Services for Adults in Higher Education.* Metuchen, N.J.: Scarecrow Press, 1971.

Thornton, R., and Mitchell, I. *Counseling the Distance Learner: A Survey of Trends and Literature.* Adelaide, Australia: Adelaide University, 1978.

University of Southern California. *Ways and Means of Strengthening Information and Counseling Services for Adult Learners.* Los Angeles: College of Continuing Education, University of Southern California, 1978.

Walz, G. R., and Benjamin, L. *Counseling Adults for Life Transitions.* Ann Arbor, Mich.: ERIC Counseling and Personnel Services Clearinghouse, 1980.

Wertheim, J. *The YES System: Why? What? How?* Bloomington: School of Continuing Studies, Indiana University, 1980.

Judith B. Wertheim is a counselor in the Division of Continuing Education, Indiana University, Bloomington.

What issues are likely to confront counselors and administrators
who want to strengthen counseling services for adult learners?

Emerging Issues in Counseling Adult Learners

Alan B. Knox

Most readers of this sourcebook are likely to be committed to the importance of continuing education counseling. The foregoing chapters describe various approaches to counseling adult learners and contain suggestions about ways in which counseling services can be strengthened. This concluding chapter highlights emerging issues and suggests initial steps that counselors and administrators could take to strengthen the counseling function.

Clients

Much of what is now known about adulthood has implications for counseling adult learners (Knox, 1977a). Some of the human development literature is focused on portions of the adult life cycle, such as young adulthood (Bocknek, 1980), middle age (Stevenson, 1977), and later maturity (Kalish, 1975). In some instances, such writings include descriptions of ways in which continuing education practitioners use generalizations about adults as learners for purposes of counseling, teaching, and program development (Knox, 1979b).

But in practice, how widespread are such understandings among practitioners who counsel and teach adult learners? How are generalizations from the professional literature combined with conclusions from assessment centers or need assessment studies or counseling interviews to identify unmet educational needs of the clientele (Pennington, 1980)? Such a detailed understanding of the clientele is especially important for agency efforts to serve hard-to-reach adults (Darkenwald and Larson, 1980).

Counselors are more likely than most people associated with adult and continuing education agencies to be familiar with the adult development literature (Goldberg, 1980). One step that counselors of adult learners could take would be to help teachers and administrators in their agency better understand adults as learners. This could be accomplished through informal conversations and distribution of reprints, as well as in staff meetings and staff development sessions. Anonymous examples from the local clientele could be combined with generalizations from the literature as a way of increasing relevance and of applying the generalizations for more responsive programming.

Assistance

There are many forms of assistance that counselors can provide to adult learners (Goldberg, 1980; Knox and Farmer, 1977). Some are widespread, such as provision of information about educational opportunities or assistance with career-related decision making. Other forms of assistance are unusual, such as group counseling sessions for preventive purposes or provision of counseling in outreach locations to attract hard-to-reach adults.

A useful question for practitioners to consider is, how comprehensive a mix of counseling services is appropriate in a specific location? Use of peer counselors may be especially effective to attract and encourage hard-to-reach adults. Use of organizational development procedures may help increase organizational support for the counseling function (Votruba, 1981). The most satisfactory mix would seem to vary with the clientele, program offerings, and other counseling services that are available. Practitioners might periodically evaluate the mix of counseling assistance for adult learners to help decide on the emphases and modifications that seem desirable in a given situation.

Media

Media and technology constitute promising resources for counseling adult learners as well as delivery of instruction. Examples include use of telephones, audiotapes, and computers (Chamberlain, 1980). But what about ethical concerns about use of such media for counseling purposes?

Traditionally, counseling has emphasized face-to-face contact in order to individualize, deal with feelings, pick up subtle cues, and guard against extreme reactions. How can the benefits of media be gained and the erosion of the main benefits of counseling be minimized? Practitioners interested in exploring innovative uses of media for counseling adult learners might conduct demonstration projects and share conclusions with colleagues.

Roles

Adults use continuing education to enhance their proficiencies in many life roles related to family, work, and community. Some writers have urged a comprehensive approach to counseling that encompasses the entire human career, including all life roles. In practice, much counseling of adult learners focuses on occupational development.

How much counseling attention to nonoccupational matters is warranted (Grotelueschen and Knox, 1979)? Practitioners might compare student preferences for counseling related to nonoccupational matters with the current occupational emphasis of counseling services. If major discrepancies are revealed, one or two might be the focus of an expanded effort. Illustrative counseling activities might emphasize developmental assistance regarding roles as consumers, family members, or users of leisure (Bolles, 1978).

Contributors

Who contributes to the counseling function? In continuing education, most counseling is performed by people who are not full-time professional counselors. Examples include administrators, teachers, paraprofessionals, and representatives of other organizations (Knox and Farmer, 1977). It is generally assumed that these various contributions to the counseling function are complementary. However, how much differentiation is desirable?

If standards of effective counseling are to be maintained, are there limits that should be recognized? At what points should peer counselors or teachers refer adult learners with severe problems to professional counselors, perhaps outside the continuing education agency? As increasing attention is being given to educational counseling by work supervisors and by instructors of returning students (Apps, 1981), it is even useful to alert adult learners to the types of counseling assistance they should expect from various categories of staff. It seems desirable for professional counselors to take the lead in helping to differentiate the various contributions to the counseling function.

Programming

All staff members associated with a continuing education agency can contribute to program development (Knox and Associates, 1980). Over the years, counselors have focused their attention on the students and have engaged very little in program development. As continuing education providers create more instructional options and greater organizational flexibility, counselors are becoming more central in the assessment of educational needs and in the selection of alternative learning activities.

In specific settings, how much input do counselors provide for program development decisions? If programming is less than desired, what existing constraints could be reduced? One step would be for counselors of adult learners to review the additional contributions that they might make to program development and to select several for which the costs to themselves are small but the benefits to the agency in the form of responsive programming are likely to be great. A promising example would be periodically to summarize unmet educational needs that emerge as a byproduct of counseling sessions and to suggest them to program administrators as a form of needs assessment to stimulate new or modified offerings.

Evaluation

There has been some evaluation of counseling services for adult learners, but not much. Practitioners who want to strengthen the counseling function can use evaluation to identify strengths and weaknesses, and to help formulate proposals for improvement (Grotelueschen, Gooler, and Knox, 1976). Examples include studies of counselor contributions to achievement and persistence of current students, as well as follow-up studies of former students (Goldberg, 1980; Knox, 1977b). Findings from local evaluation studies, combined with conclusions from pertinent evaluation studies conducted elsewhere, can enable practitioners to be persuasive advocates for improvement of counseling services for adult learners (Knox, 1979c).

Marketing

Some continuing education agencies have coordinated counseling and marketing activities. Examples of such coordination include featuring a counseling office as a single door to an agency with decentralized offerings and having counselors identify human interest stories that personalize benefits of continuing education participation.

How widespread are such close connections between continuing education counseling and marketing? How effective are they for the clientele as well as the agency? What are the advantages and disadvantages of such coordination? Practitioners might analyze current relationships between counseling and marketing activities in their agency and perhaps propose ways to strengthen those relationships (Kotler, 1974).

Providers

The increased number of continuing education providers in recent years has contributed to both heightened competition and greater opportunities for collaboration. A related development has been the emergence of community-based educational brokering offices (Heffernan, Macy, and Vickers, 1976).

Relationships among providers regarding counseling services has become a major issue that confronts practitioners. What functions are best performed by counselors associated with a provider agency, and what functions are best performed by counselors associated with an educational brokering office? How feasible is long-term support for educational brokering offices? How can practitioners establish and maintain connections among agencies that can facilitate the counseling function? A useful starting point would be to strengthen the referral process.

Literature

The professional literature on counseling adult learners is growing. Familiarity with this literature enables counselors to benefit from the experience of others (Knox, 1979a), which would appear to be a resource and hardly an issue. The issue has to do with the lack of impact that this literature has on practice. Most people who counsel adult learners do so part-time, and they usually are unfamiliar with the pertinent professional literature. Two challenges confront practioners. One is to contribute to the professional literature so that others can benefit from their experience. The second is to encourage those who counsel adult learners to use the professional literature to enhance their counseling proficiencies (Goldberg, 1980).

Support

A long-standing issue has been inadequate policy and administrative and financial support for the continuing education counseling function (Knox and Associates, 1980). Most continuing education agencies have no professional counselors and the counseling assistance provided by administrators and teachers is uneven. In agencies with counseling staff, the level of desirability of counseling services as perceived by counselors tends to be higher than that perceived by administrators and policy makers. Part of the reason is that the counseling function has been perceived as something done by counselors, as a source of expense, and as a benefit to adult learners with problems. By contrast, in agencies with strong counseling efforts the counseling function is perceived as a responsibility of all staff members, professional counselors coordinate such efforts, counseling is related to the marketing function and contributes to enrollment and financial stability, and a broad range of services are provided that benefit most participants. The resolution of most of the foregoing issues depends on practitioners building and maintaining support for the counseling function. Conversely, evidence of progress regarding the foregoing issues can be instrumental in strengthening support for counseling services for adult learners.

References

Apps, J. *Adult Learner on Campus*. Chicago: Follett, 1981.
Bocknek, G. *The Young Adult*. Monterey, Calif.: Brooks/Cole, 1980.
Bolles, R. N. *The Three Boxes of Life*. Berkeley, Calif.: Ten Speed Press, 1978.

108

Chamberlain, M. N. (Ed.). *New Directions for Continuing Education: Providing Continuing Education by Media and Technology,* no. 5. San Francisco: Jossey-Bass, 1980.

Darkenwald, G. G., and Larson, G. A. (Eds.). *New Directions for Continuing Education: Reaching Hard-to-Reach Adults,* no. 8. San Francisco: Jossey-Bass, 1980.

Goldberg, J. C. "Counseling the Adult Learner: A Selective Review of the Literature." *Adult Education,* 1980, *30* (2), 67–81.

Grotelueschen, A. D., Gooler, D. D., and Knox, A. B. *Evaluation in Adult Basic Education: How and Why.* Danville, Ill: Interstate, 1976.

Grotelueschen, A. D., and Knox, A. B. *Adult Participation in Nonoccupational Lifelong Learning: Background for National Policy Formulation.* Occasional Paper No. 6. Urbana: Office of the Study of Continuing Professional Education, University of Illinois, 1979.

Heffernan, J. M., Macy, F. V., and Vickers, D. F. *Educational Brokering: A New Service for Adult Learners.* Syracuse, N.Y.: National Center for Educational Brokering, 1976.

Kalish, R. A. *Late Adulthood: Perspectives on Human Development.* Monterey, Calif.: Brooks/Cole, 1975.

Knox, A. B. *Adult Development and Learning: A Handbook on Individual Growth and Competence in the Adult Years for Education and the Helping Professions.* San Francisco: Jossey-Bass, 1977a.

Knox, A. B. *Current Research Needs Related to Systematic Learning by Adults.* Occasional Paper No. 4. Urbana: Office of the Study of Continuing Professional Education, University of Illinois, 1977b.

Knox, A. B. (Ed.). *New Directions for Continuing Education: Assessing the Impact of Continuing Education,* no. 3. San Francisco: Jossey-Bass, 1979a.

Knox, A. B. (Ed.). *New Directions for Continuing Education: Enhancing Proficiencies of Continuing Educators,* no. 1. San Francisco: Jossey-Bass, 1979b.

Knox, A. B. (Ed.). *New Directions for Continuing Education: Programming for Adults Facing Mid-Life Change,* no. 2. San Francisco: Jossey-Bass, 1979c.

Knox, A. B., and Associates. *Developing, Administering, and Evaluating Adult Education.* San Francisco: Jossey-Bass, 1980.

Knox, A. B., and Farmer, H. S. "Overview of Counseling and Information Services for Adult Learners." *International Review of Education,* 1977, *23* (4), 387–414.

Kotler, P. *Marketing for Non-Profit Organizations.* Englewood Cliffs, N.J.: Prentice-Hall, 1974.

Pennington, F. C. (Ed.). *New Directions for Continuing Education: Assessing Educational Needs of Adults,* no. 7. San Francisco: Jossey-Bass, 1980.

Stevenson, J. L. *Issues and Crises During Middlescence.* New York: Appleton-Century-Crofts, 1977.

Votruba, J. *New Directions for Continuing Education: Internal Support for Continuing Education,* no. 9. San Francisco: Jossey-Bass, 1981.

Alan B. Knox is professor of continuing education at the University of Illinois at Urbana–Champaign.

Index

New Directions Quarterly Sourcebooks

New Directions for Continuing Education is one of several distinct series of quarterly sourcebooks published by Jossey-Bass. The sourcebooks in each series are designed to serve both as *convenient compendiums* of the latest knowledge and practical experience on their topics and as *long-life reference tools.*

One-year, four-sourcebook subscriptions for each series cost $18 for individuals (when paid by personal check) and $30 for institutions, libraries, and agencies. Single copies of earlier sourcebooks are available at $6.95 each *prepaid* (or $7.95 each when *billed*).

A complete listing is given below of current and past sourcebooks in the *New Directions for Continuing Education* series. The titles and editors-in-chief of the other series are also listed. To subscribe, or to receive further information, write: New Directions Subscriptions, Jossey-Bass Inc., Publishers, 433 California Street, San Francisco, California 94104.

New Directions for Continuing Education
Alan B. Knox, Editor-in-Chief
1979: 1. *Enhancing Proficiencies of Continuing Educators,*
           Alan B. Knox
        2. *Programming for Adults Facing Mid-Life Change,* Alan B. Knox
        3. *Assessing the Impact of Continuing Education,* Alan B. Knox
        4. *Attracting Able Instructors of Adults,* M. Alan Brown,
           Harlan G. Copeland
1980: 5. *Providing Continuing Education by Media and Technology,*
           Martin N. Chamberlain
        6. *Teaching Adults Effectively,* Alan B. Knox
        7. *Assessing Educational Needs of Adults,* Floyd C. Pennington
        8. *Reaching Hard-to-Reach Adults,* Gordon G. Darkenwald,
           Gordon A. Larson
1981: 9. *Strengthening Internal Support for Continuing Education,*
           James C. Votruba

New Directions for Child Development
William Damon, Editor-in-Chief

New Directions for College Learning Assistance
Kurt V. Lauridsen, Editor-in-Chief

New Directions for Community Colleges
Arthur M. Cohen, Editor-in-Chief
Florence B. Brawer, Associate Editor

New Directions for Exceptional Children
James J. Gallagher, Editor-in-Chief

New Directions for Experiential Learning
Pamela J. Tate, Editor-in-Chief
Morris T. Keeton, Consulting Editor

New Directions for Higher Education
JB Lon Hefferlin, Editor-in-Chief

New Directions for Institutional Advancement
A. Westley Rowland, Editor-in-Chief

New Directions for Institutional Research
Marvin W. Peterson, Editor-in-Chief

New Directions for Mental Health Services
H. Richard Lamb, Editor-in-Chief

New Directions for Methodology of Social and Behavioral Science
Donald W. Fiske, Editor-in-Chief

New Directions for Program Evaluation
Scarvia B. Anderson, Editor-in-Chief

New Directions for Student Services
Ursula Delworth and Gary R. Hanson, Editors-in-Chief

New Directions for Teaching and Learning
Kenneth E. Eble and John F. Noonan, Editors-in-Chief

New Directions for Testing and Measurement
William B. Schrader, Editor-in-Chief

8592